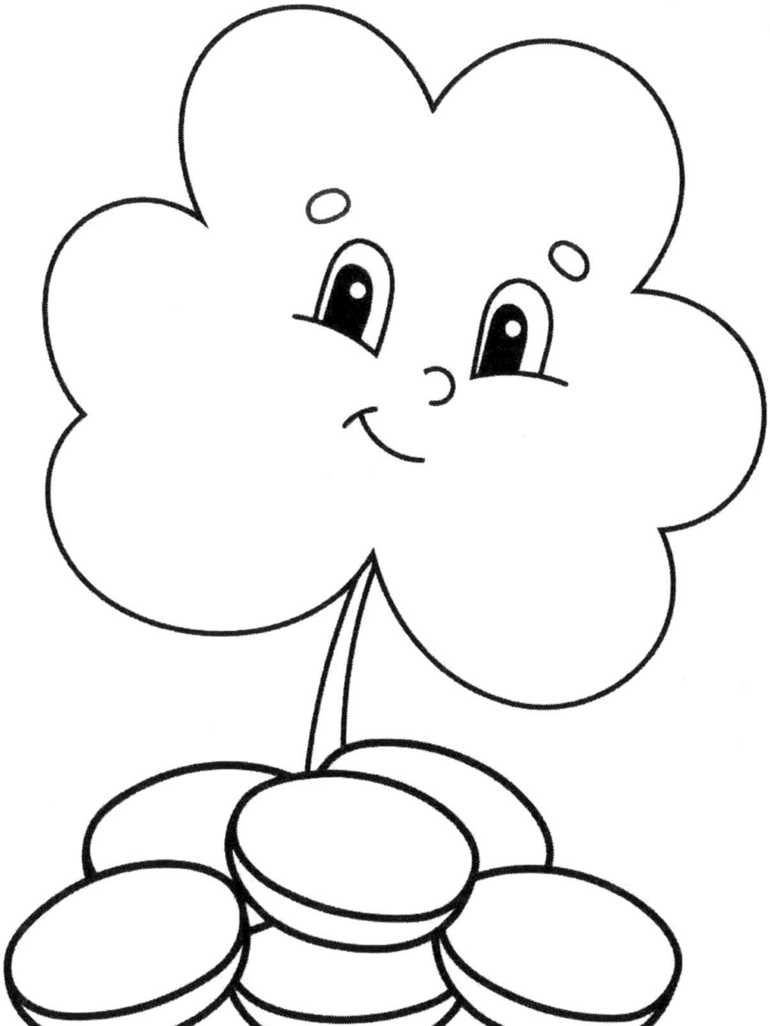

THIS BOOK BELONGS TO

COLOR TEST PAGE

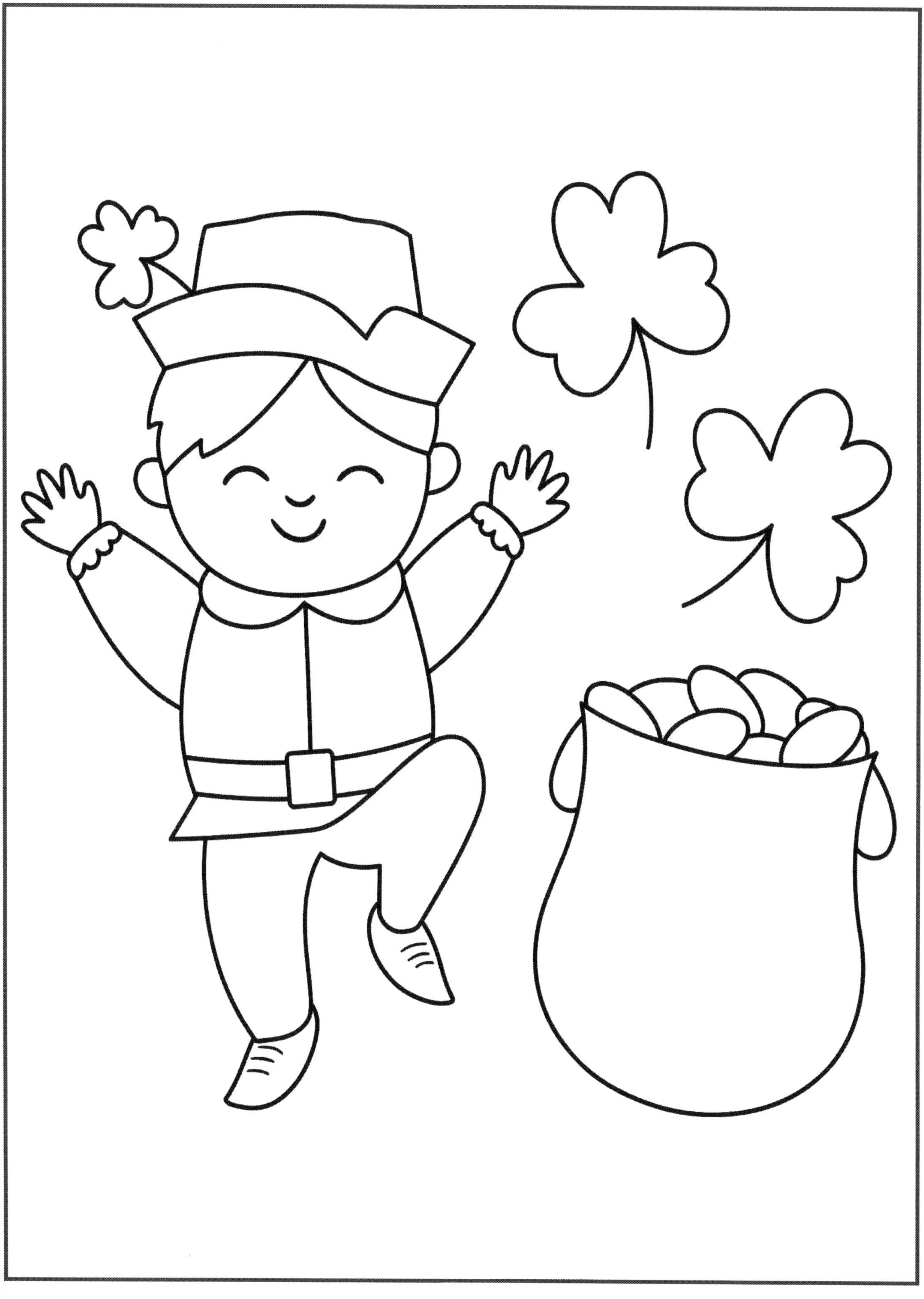

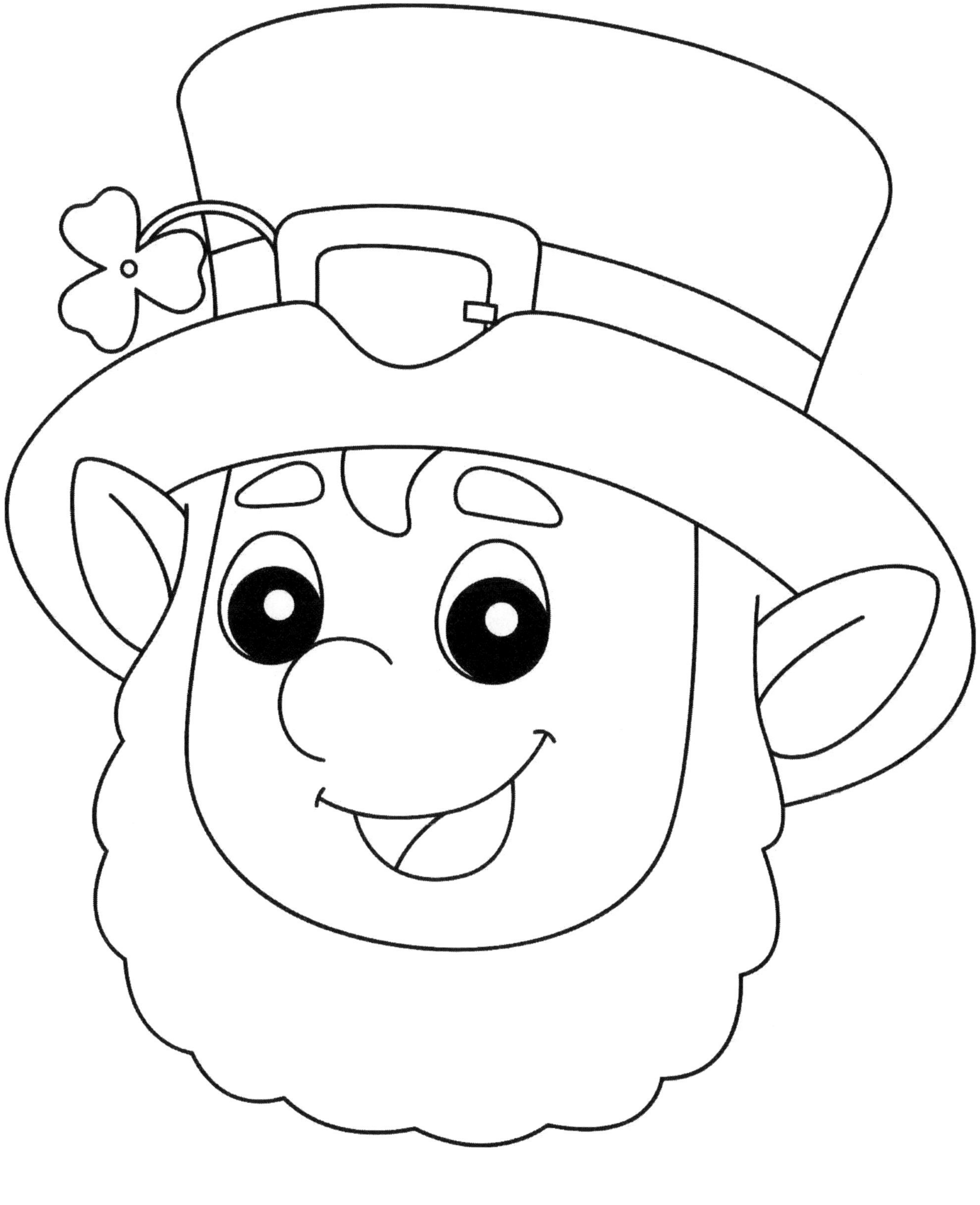

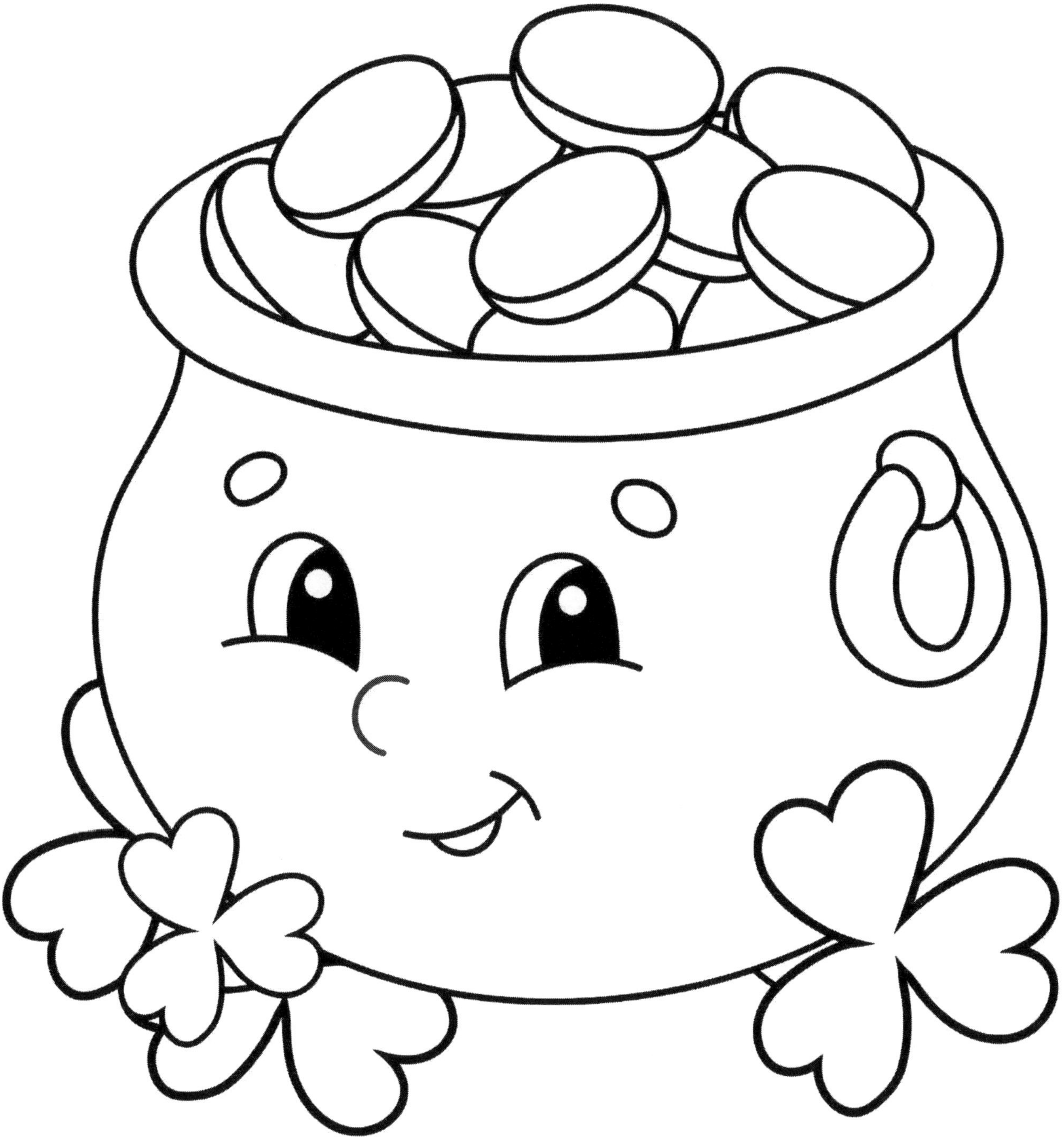

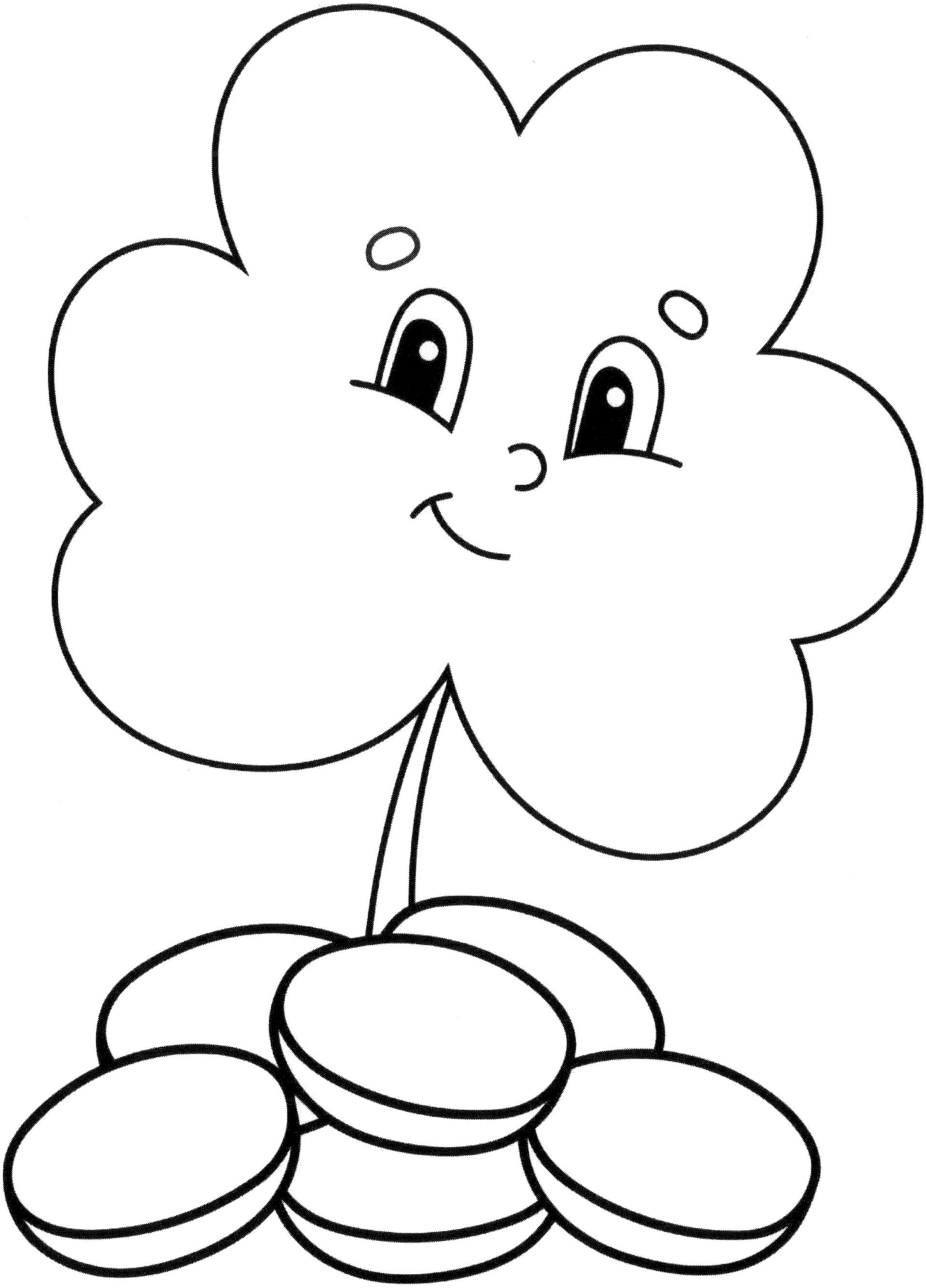

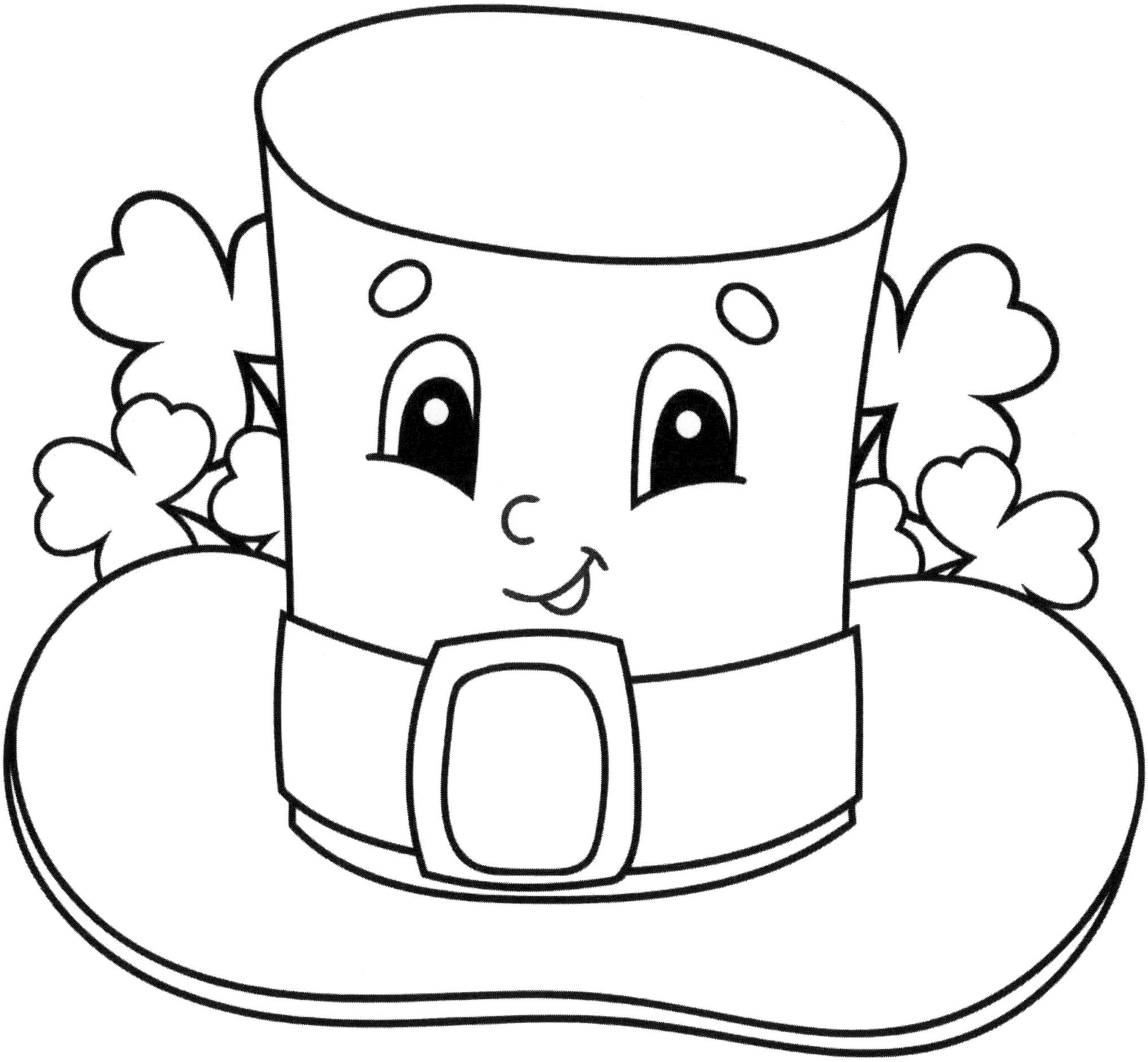

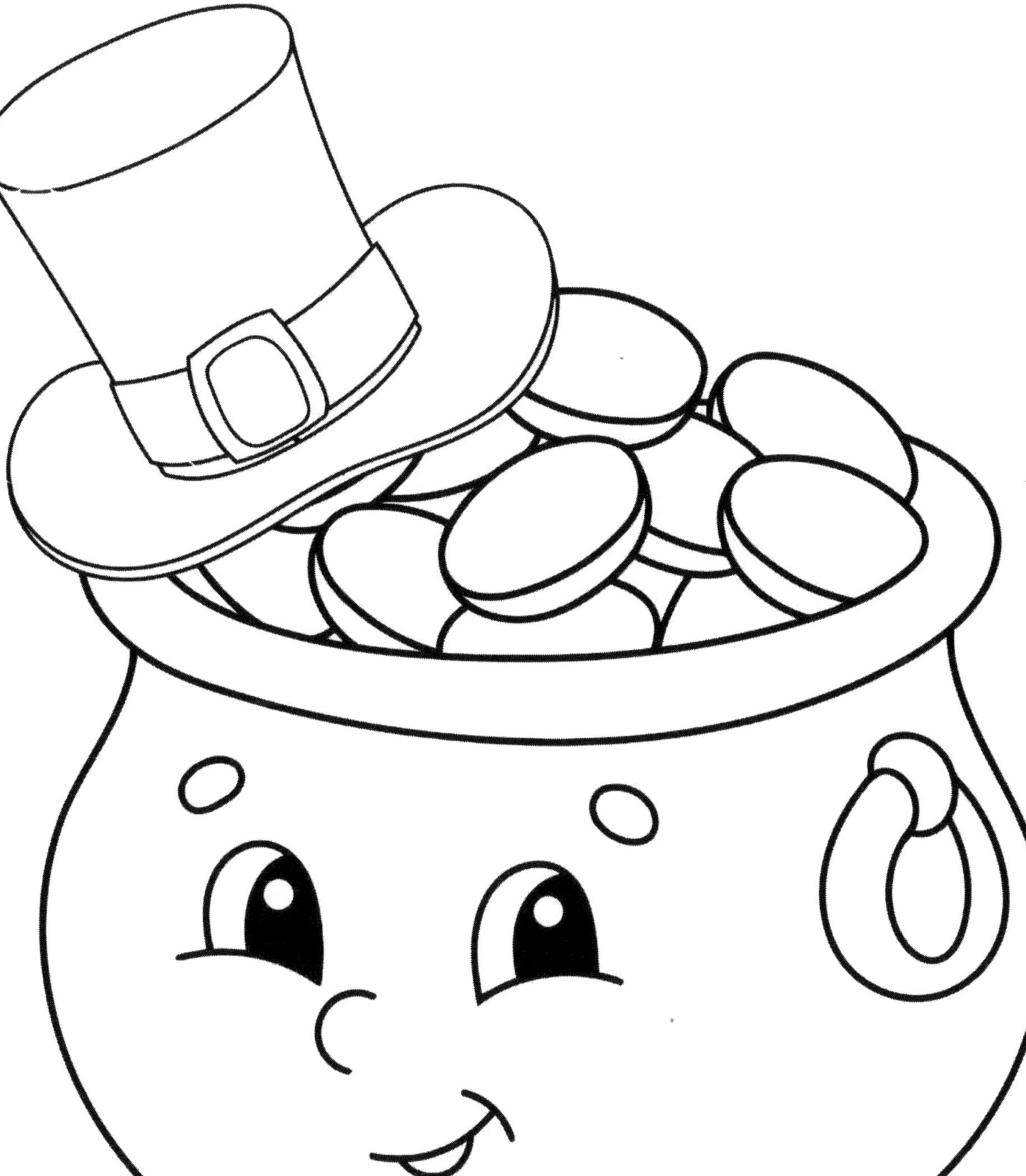

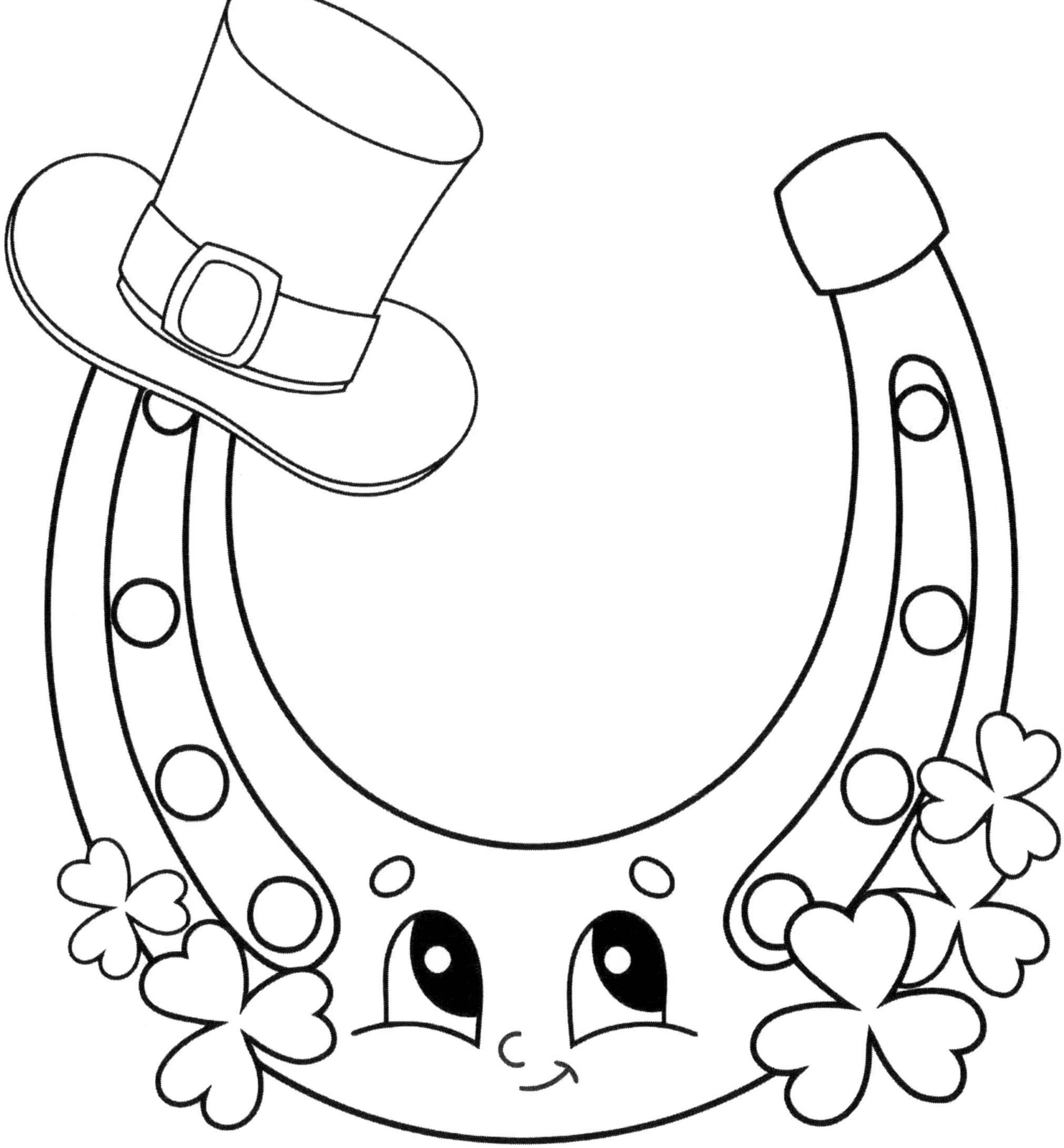

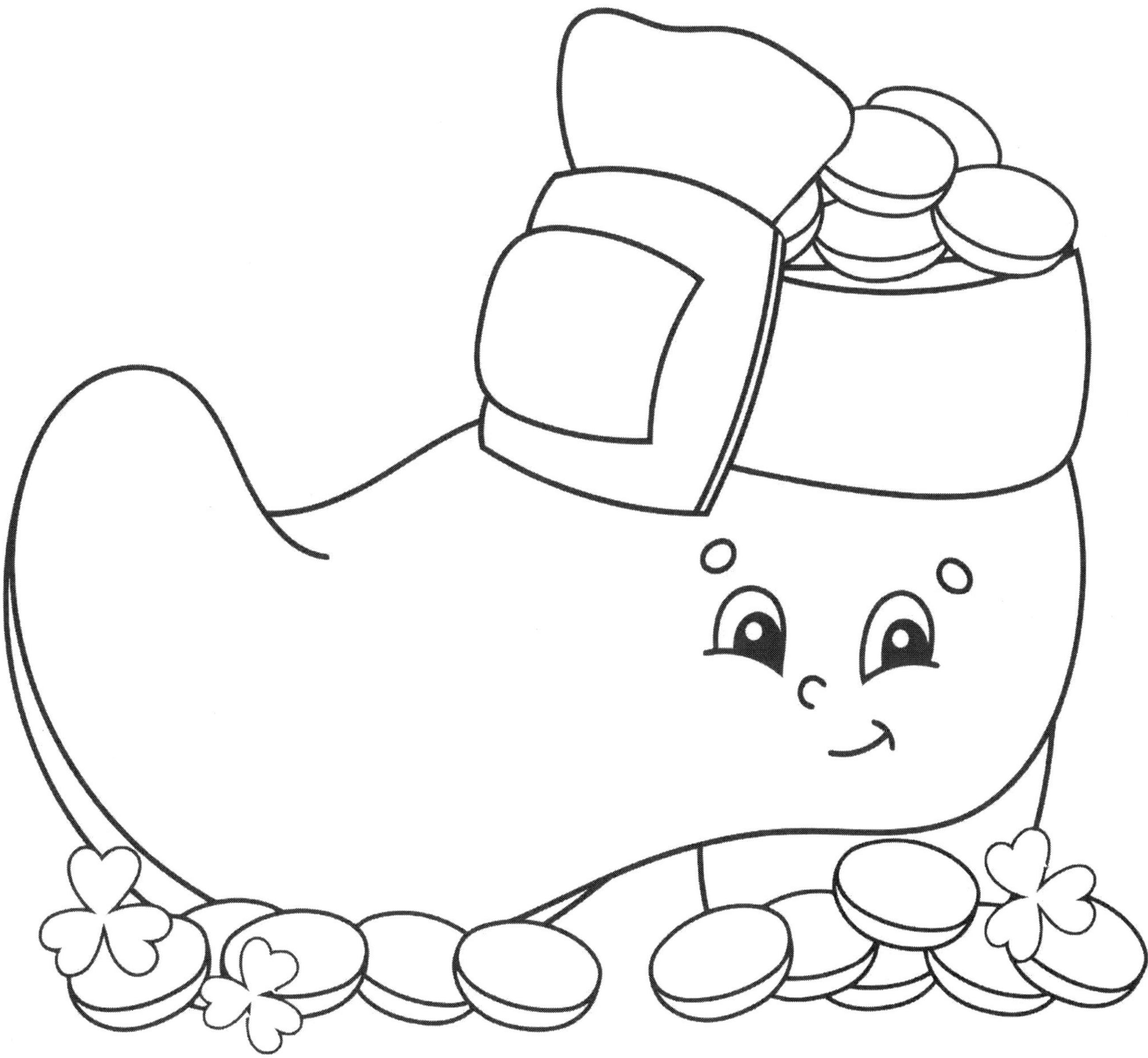

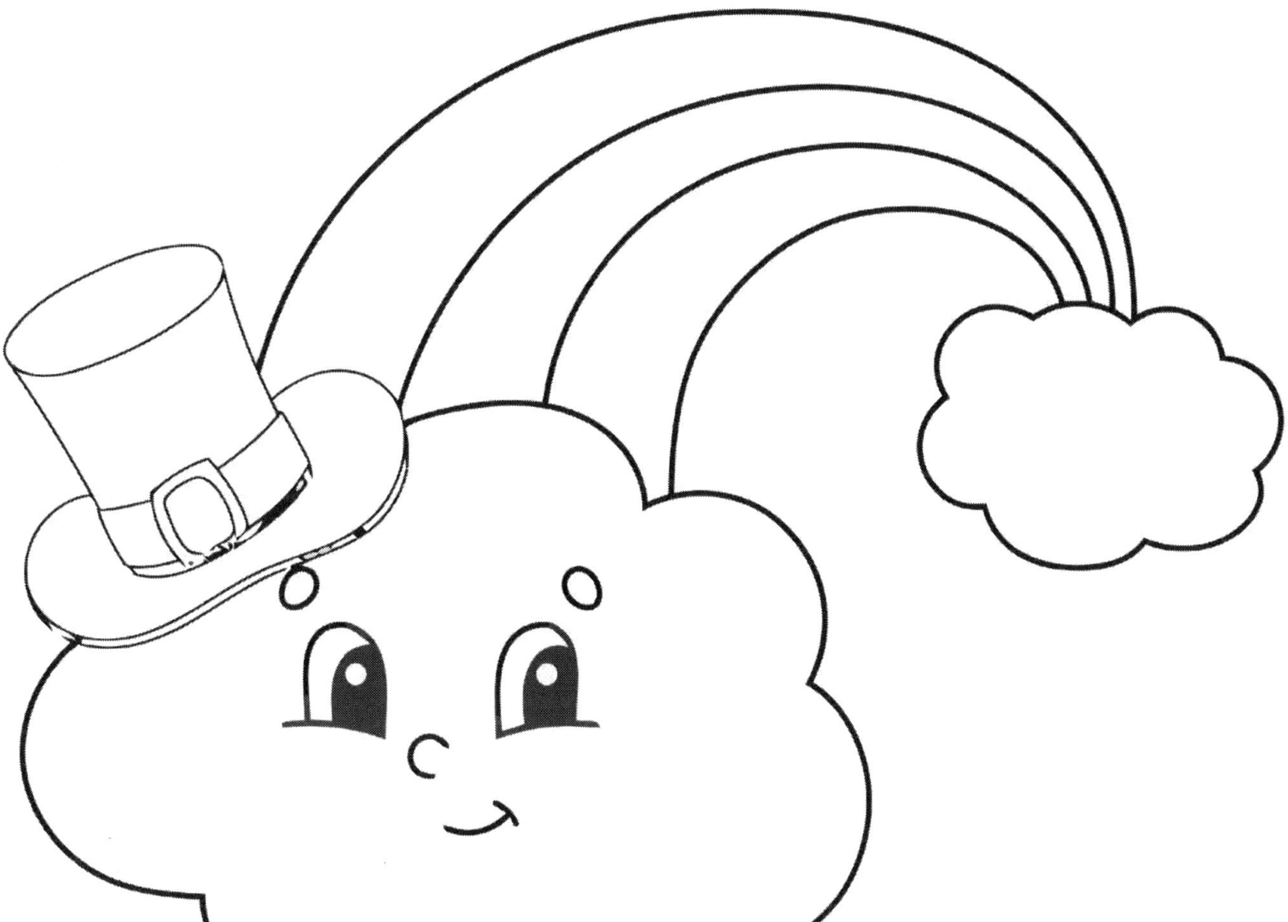

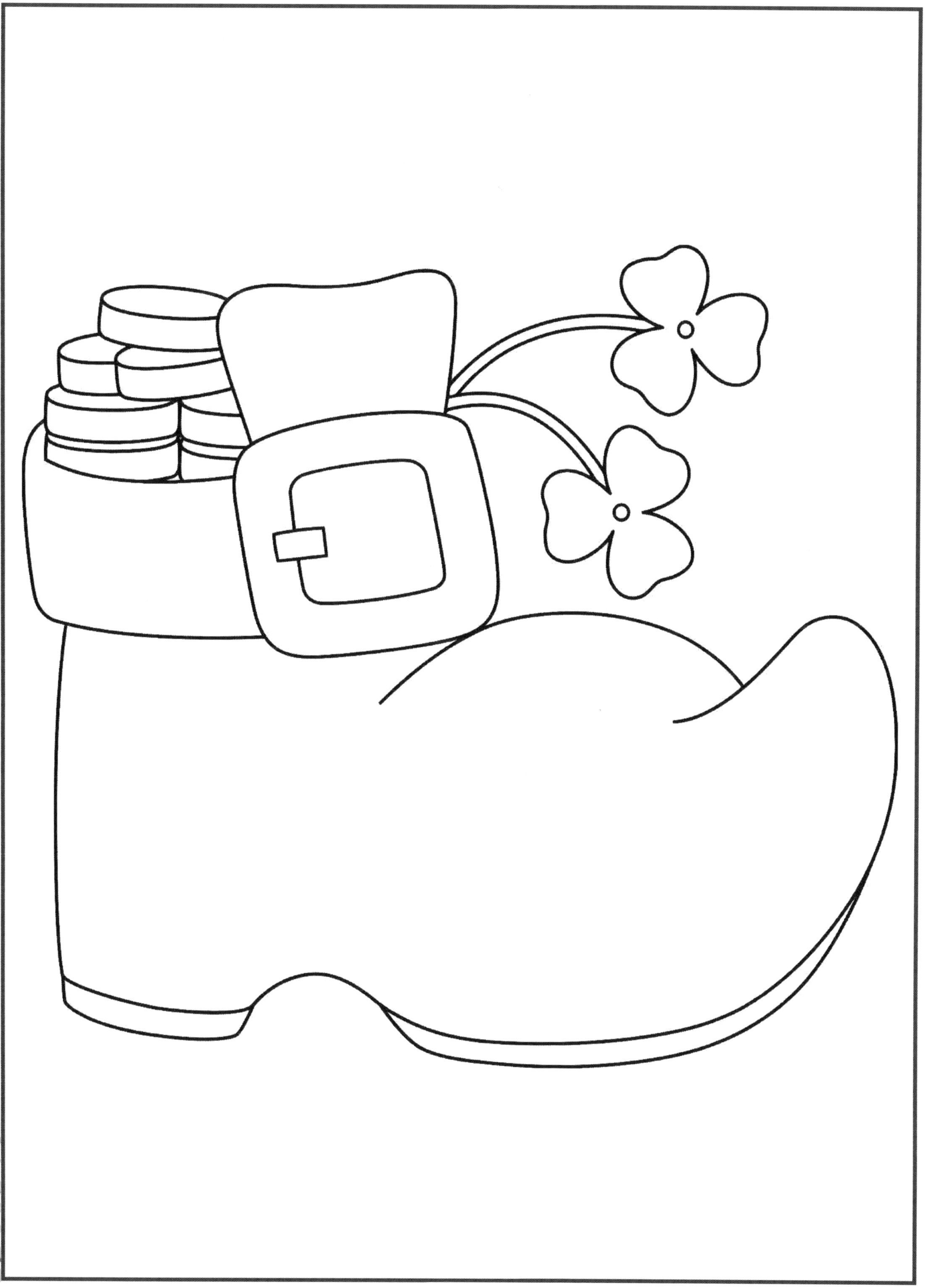

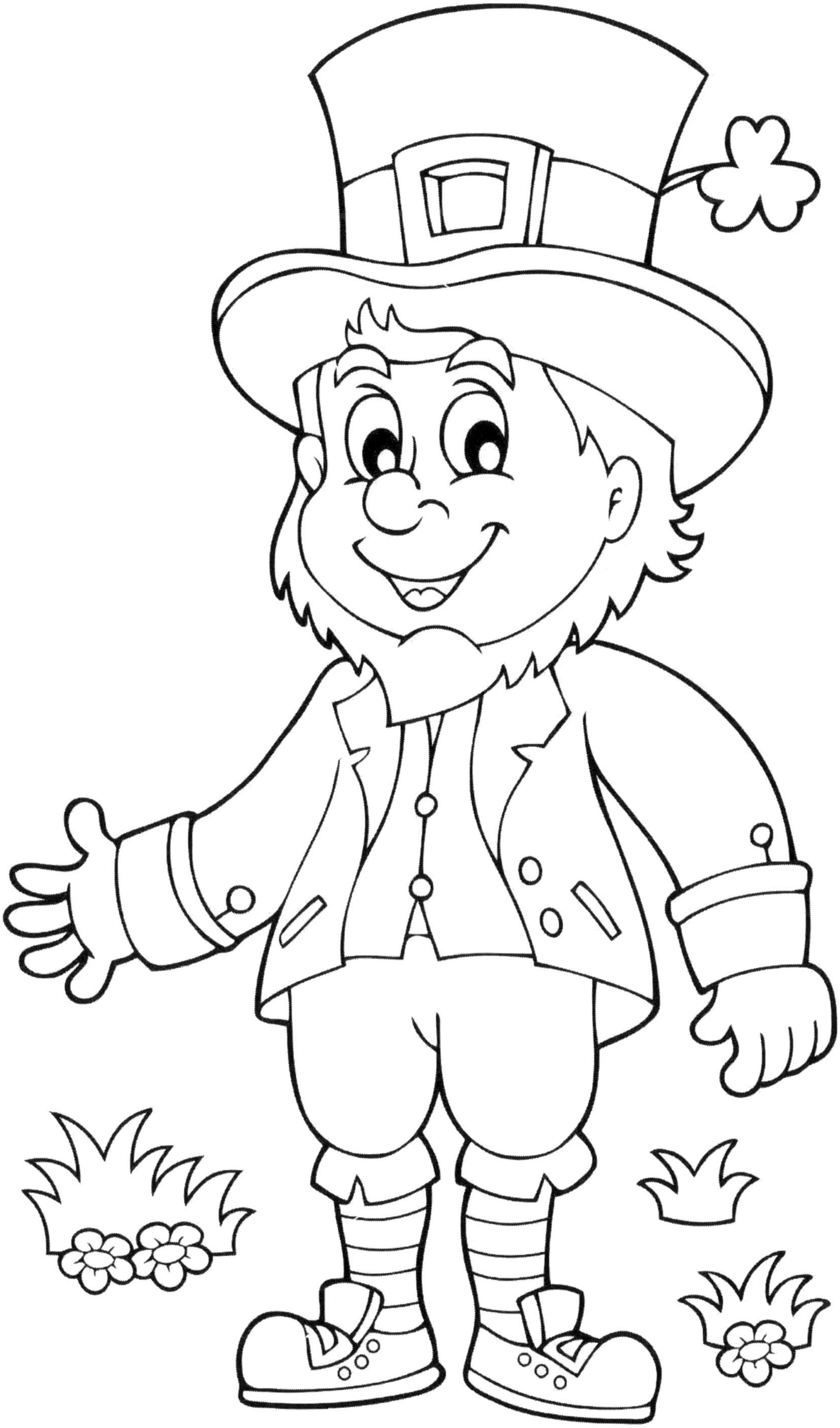

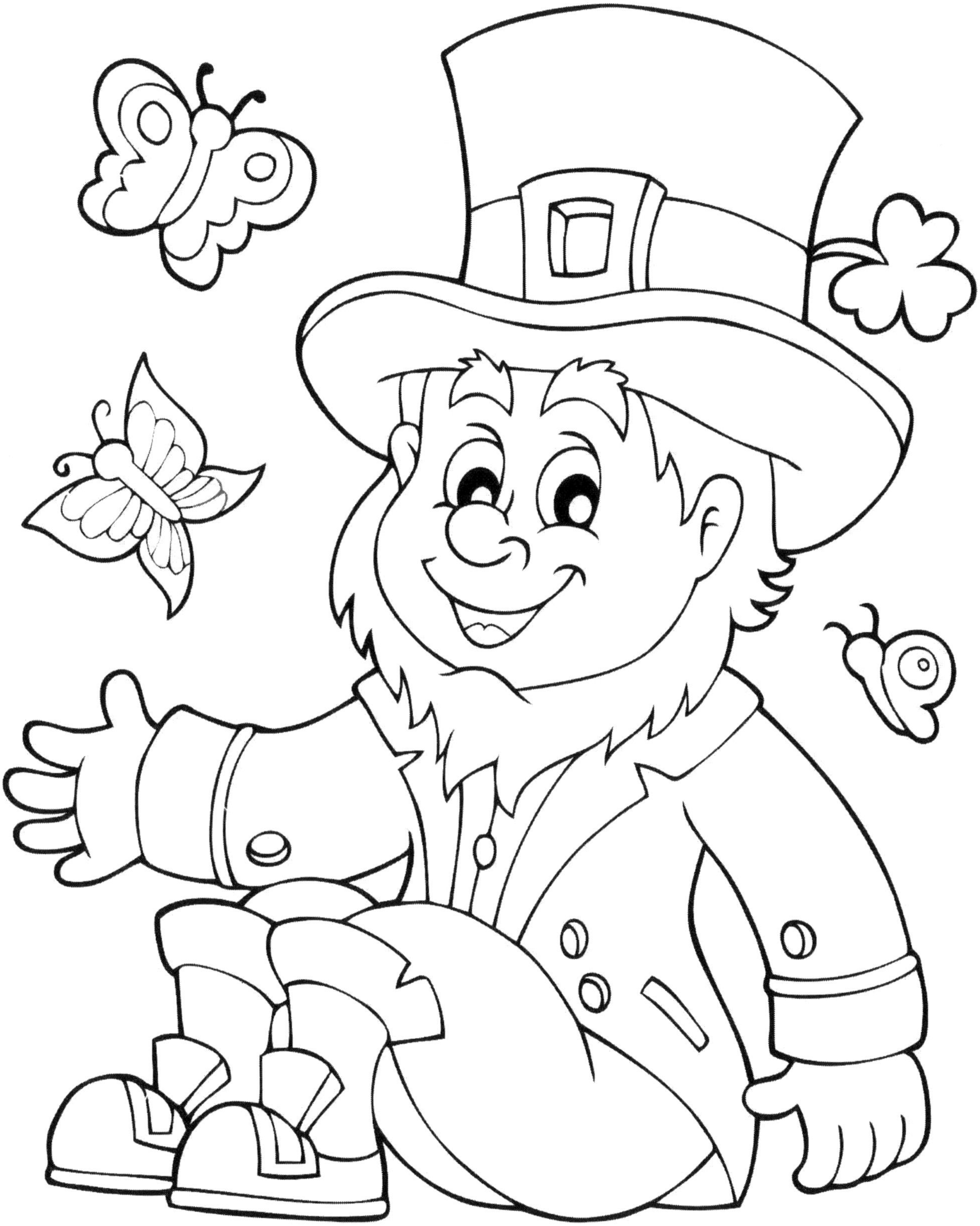

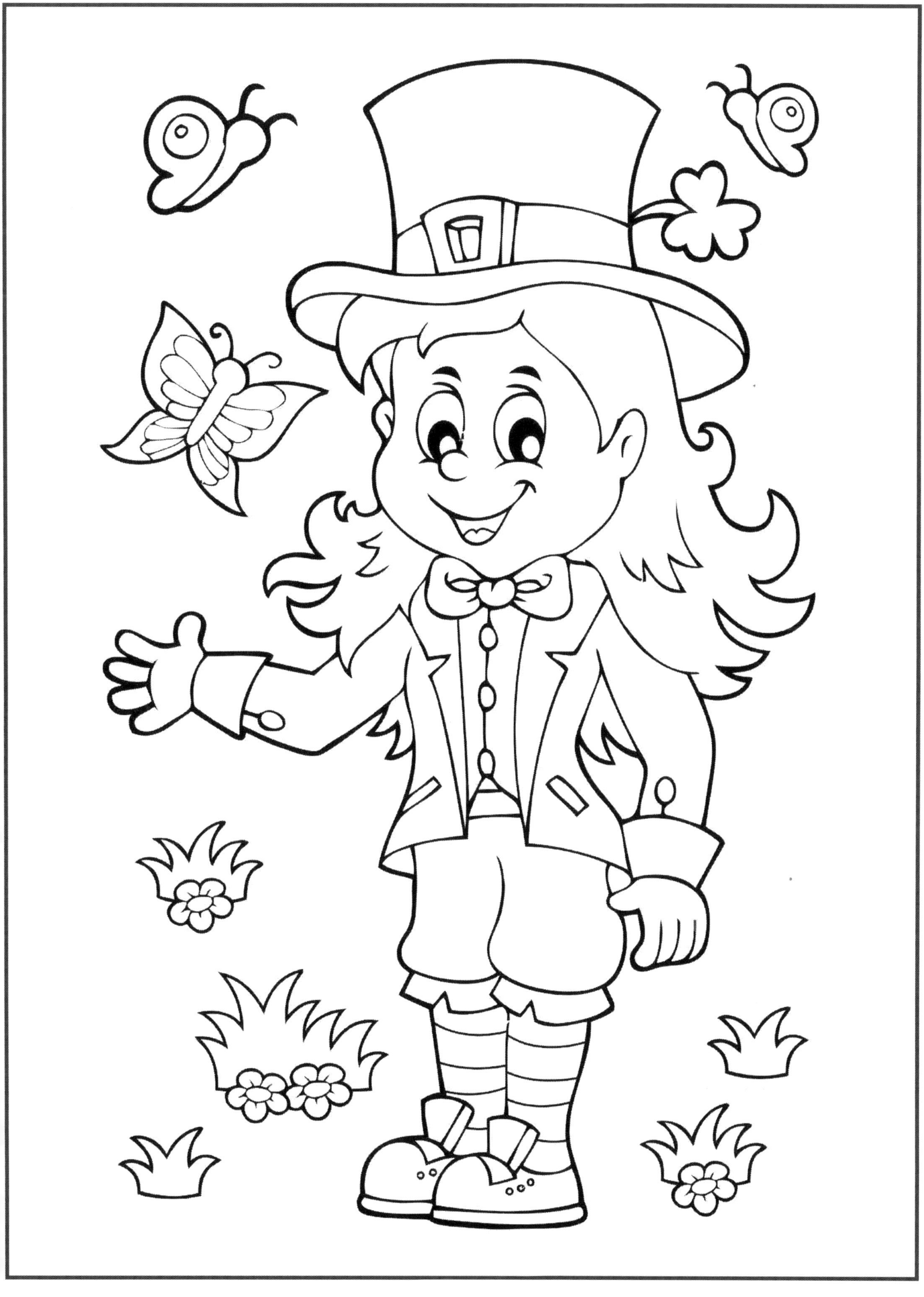

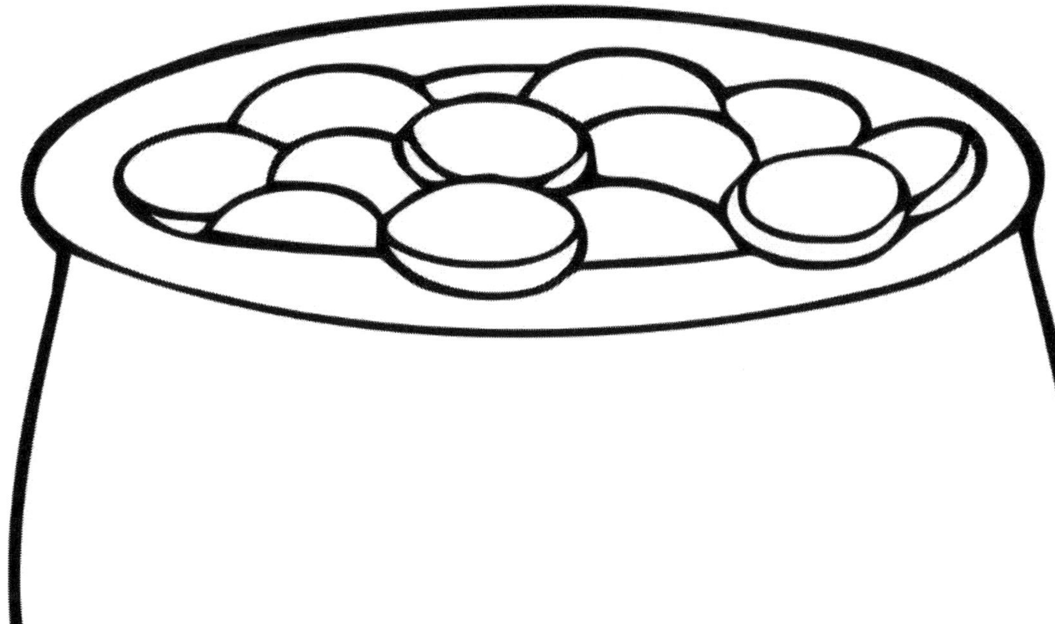

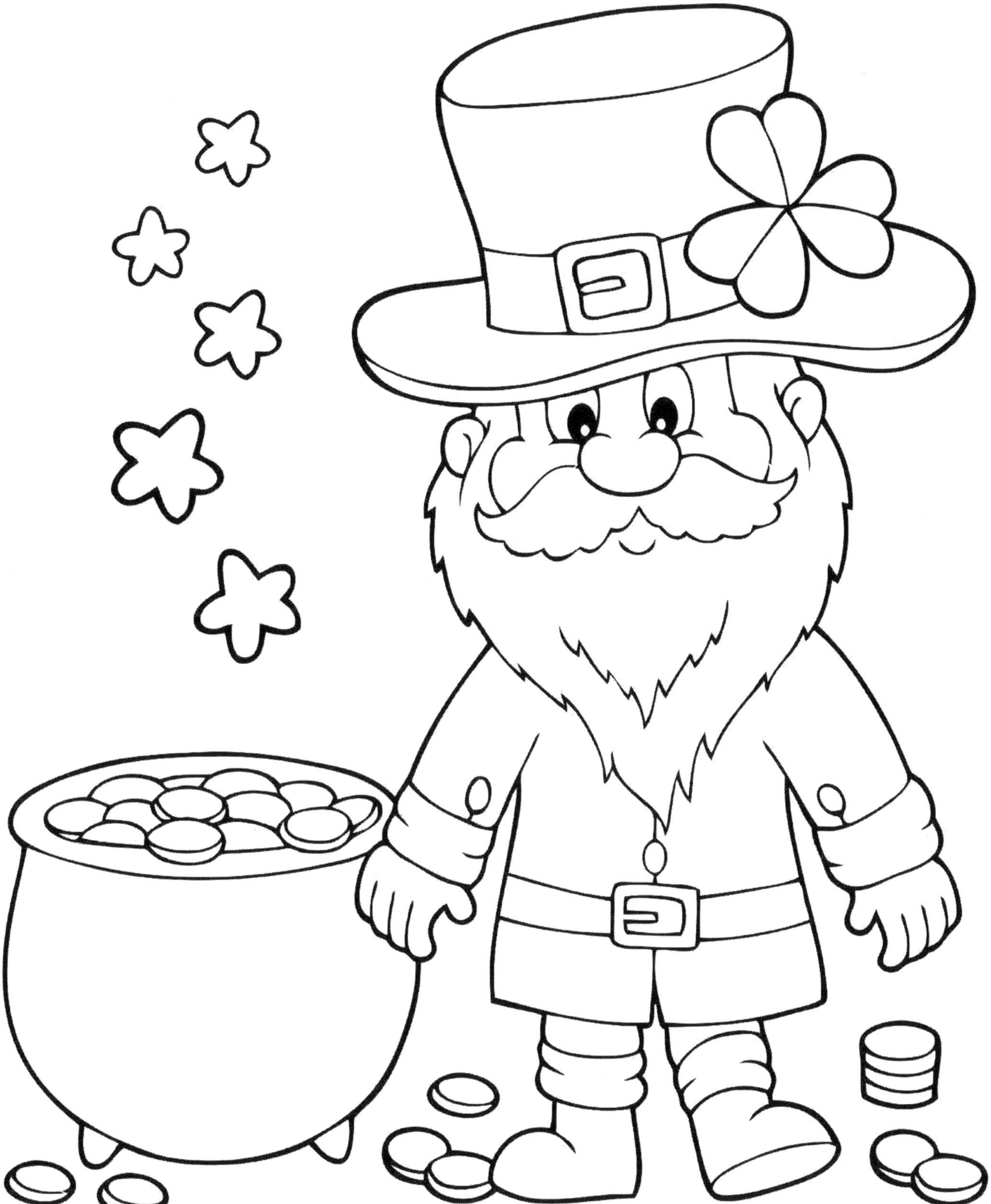

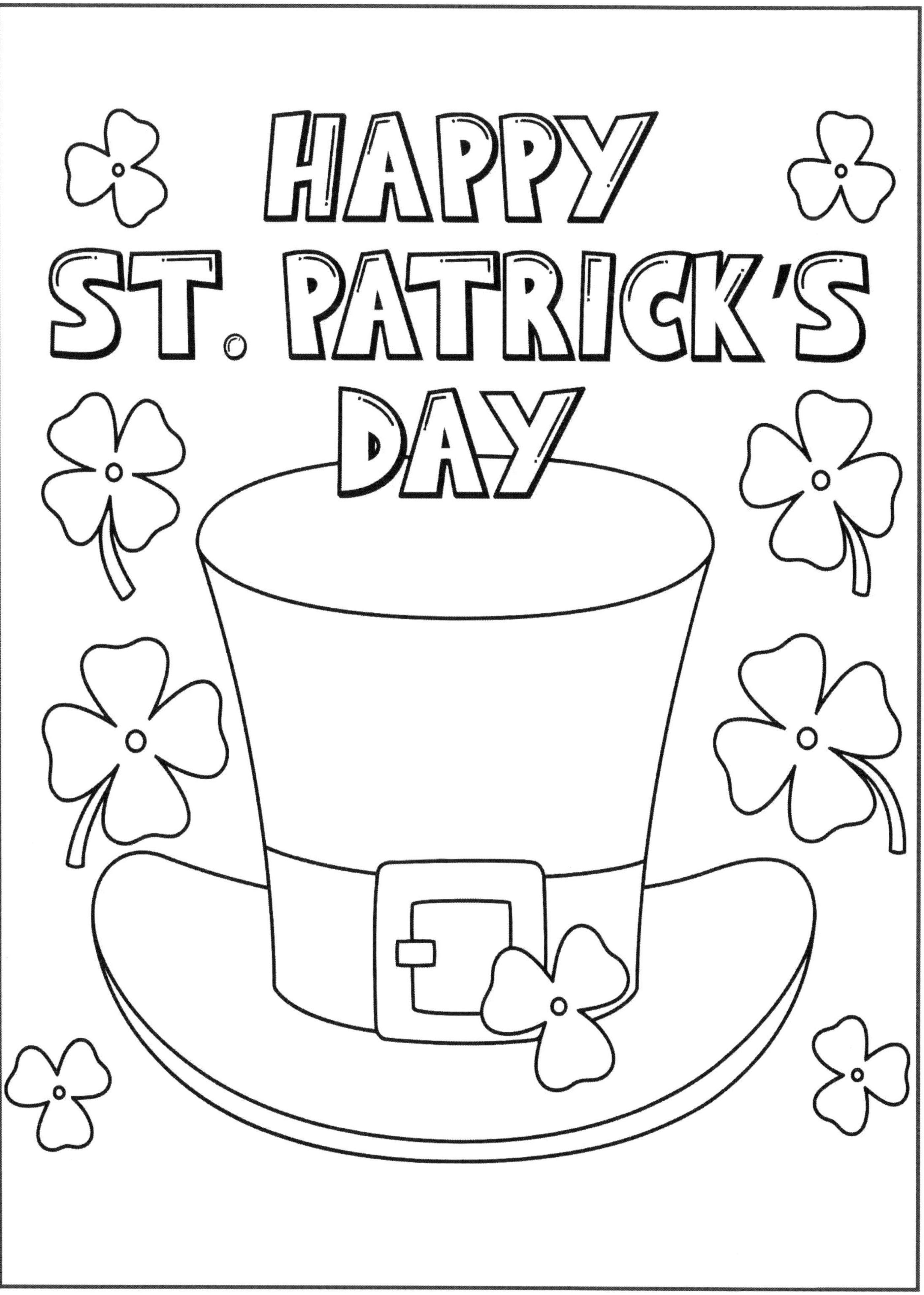
HAPPY
ST. PATRICK'S
DAY

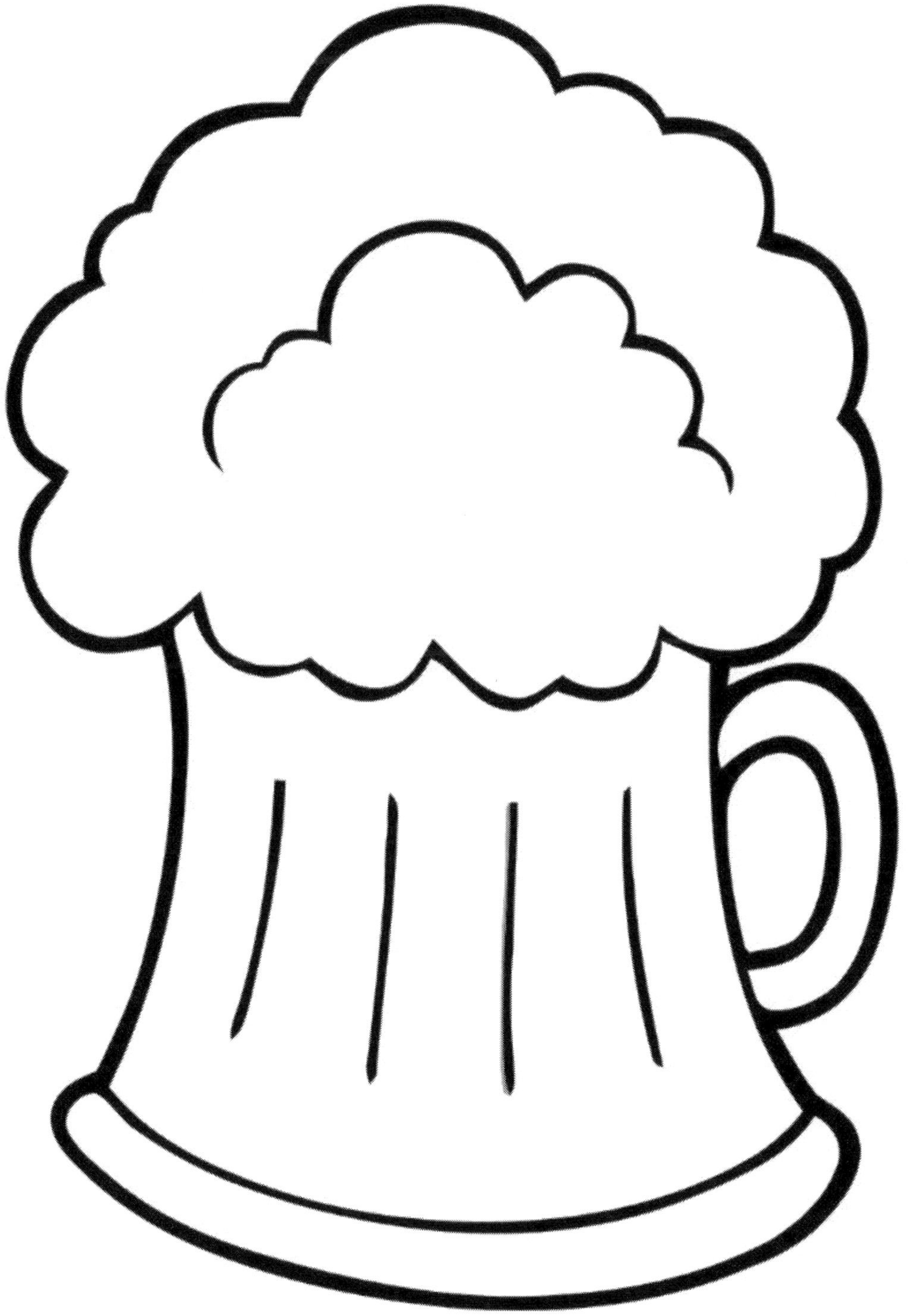

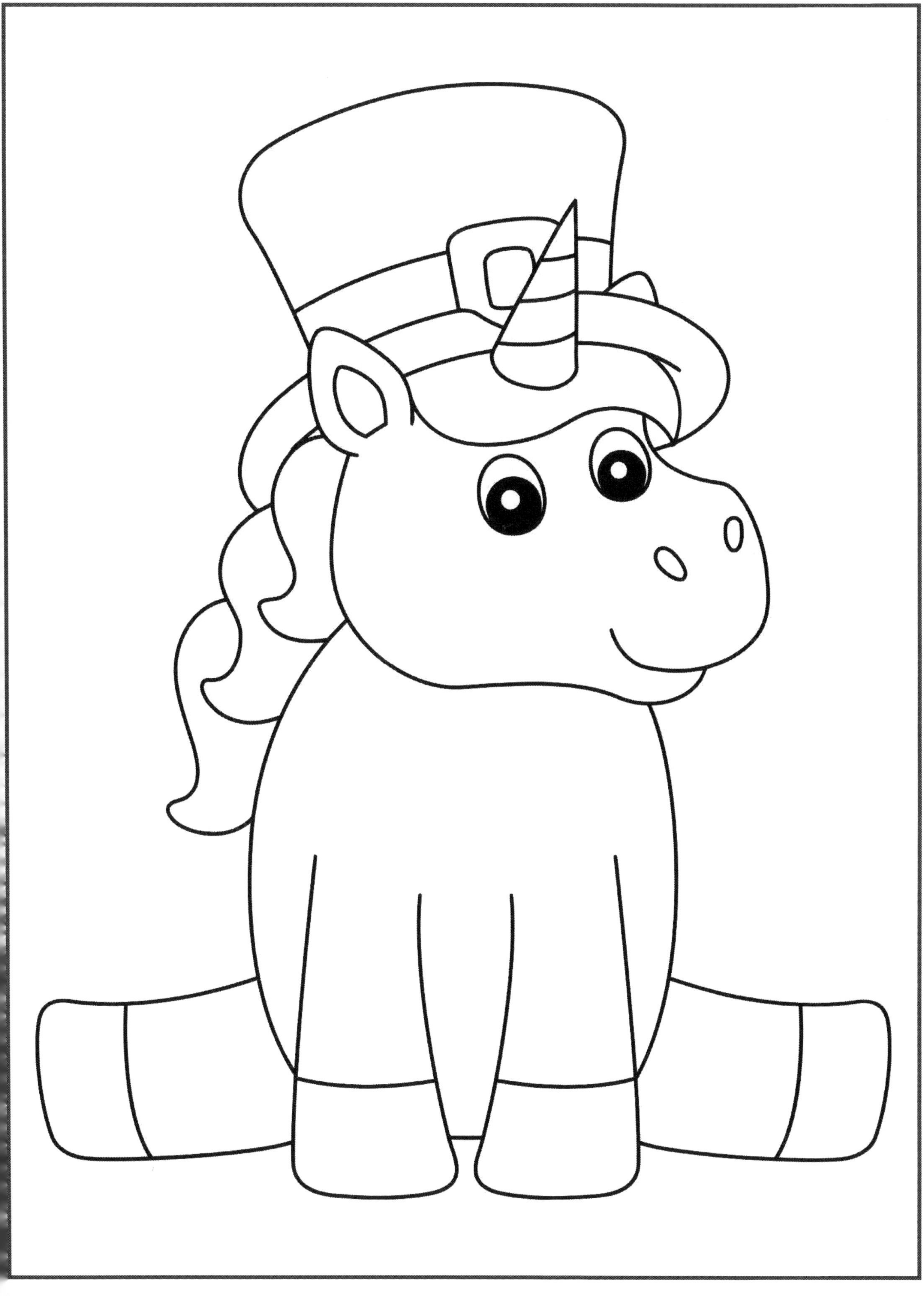

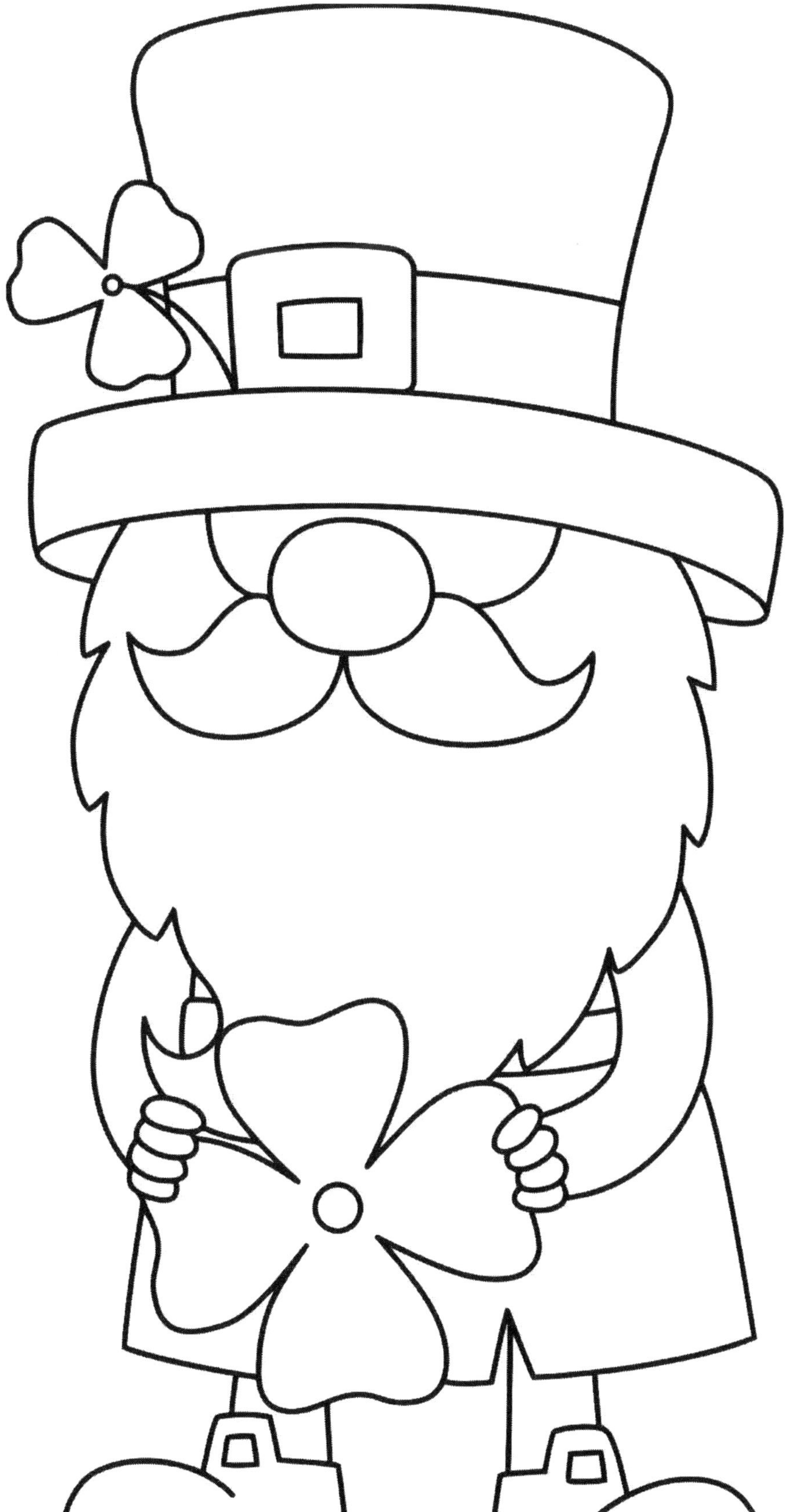

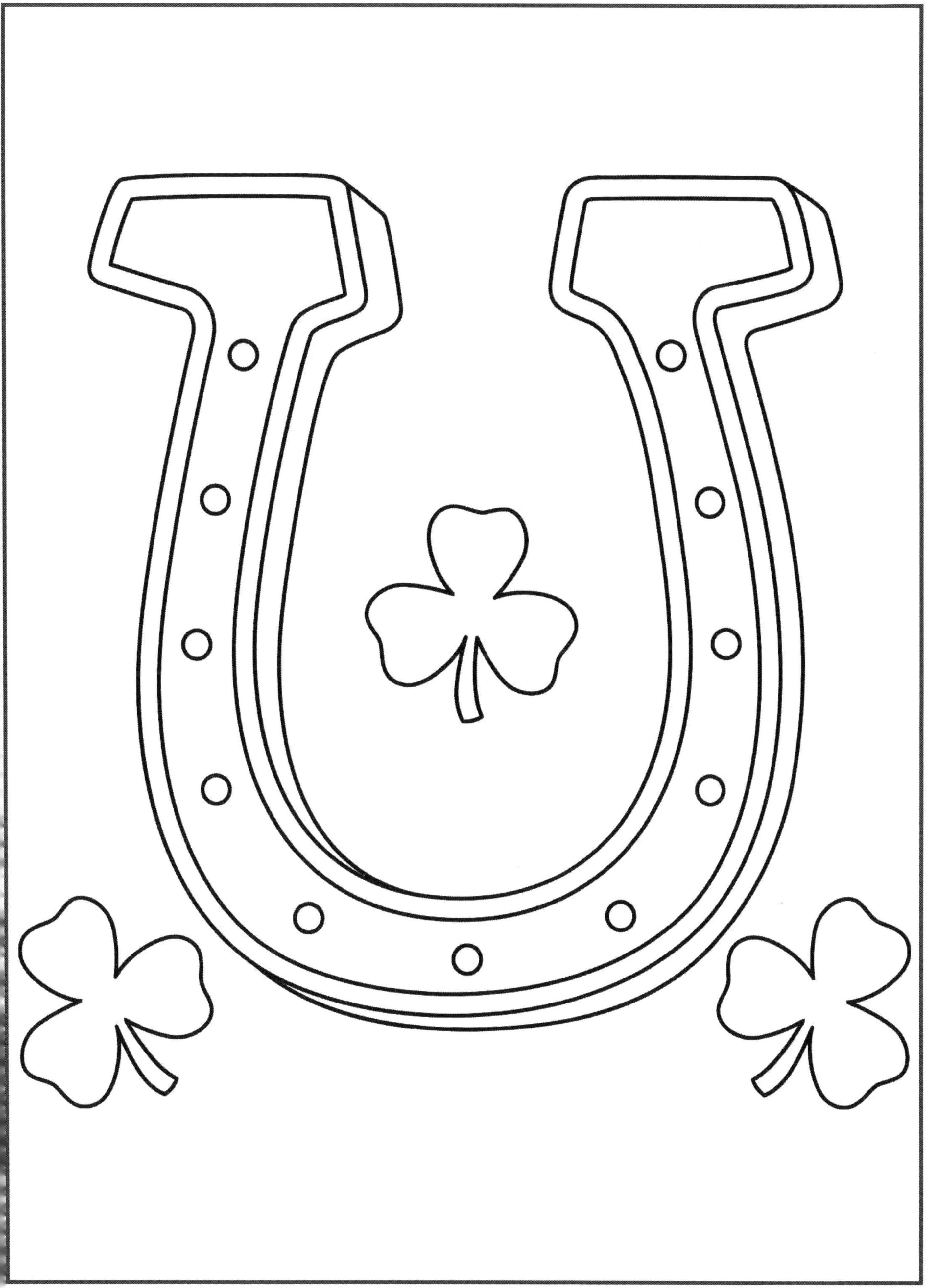

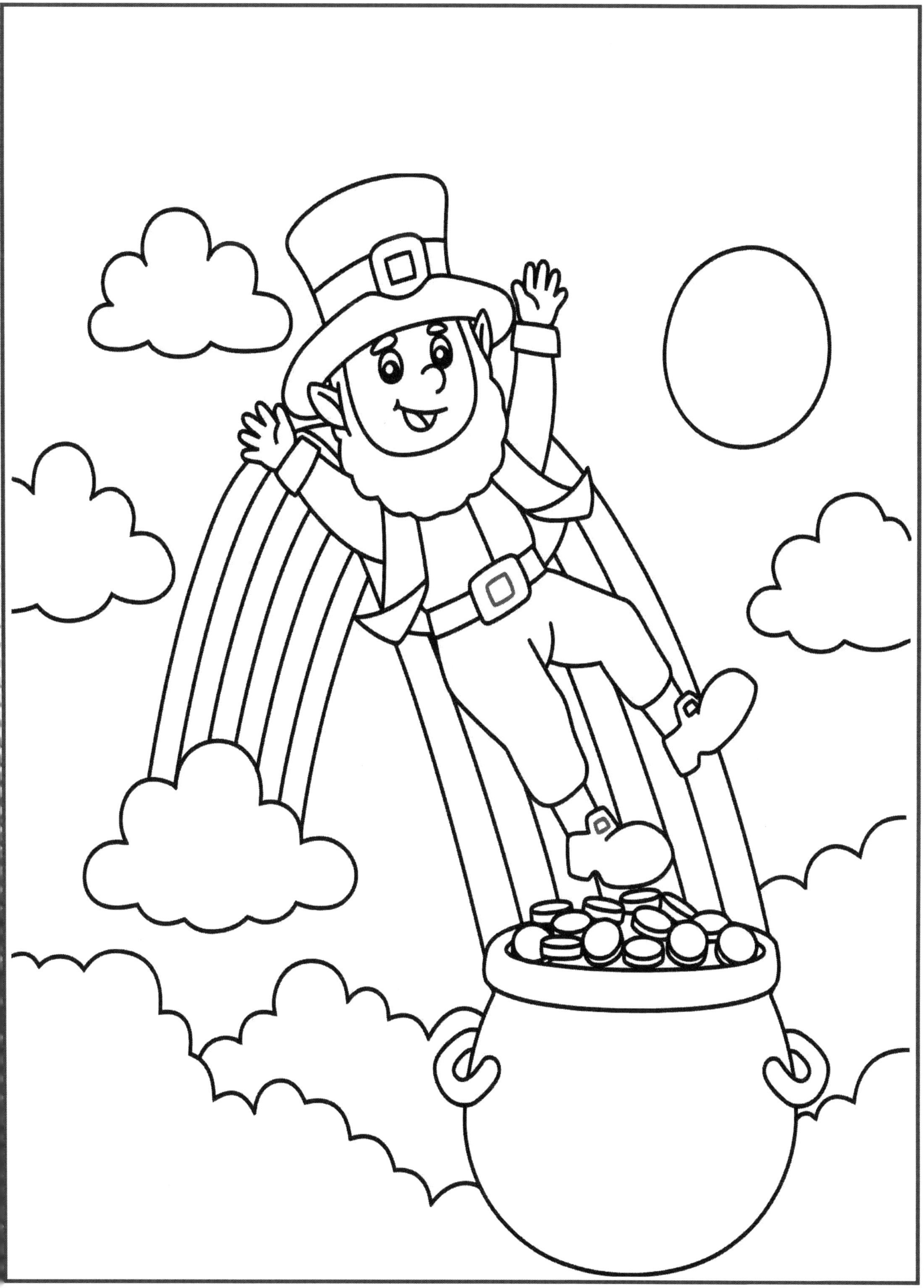

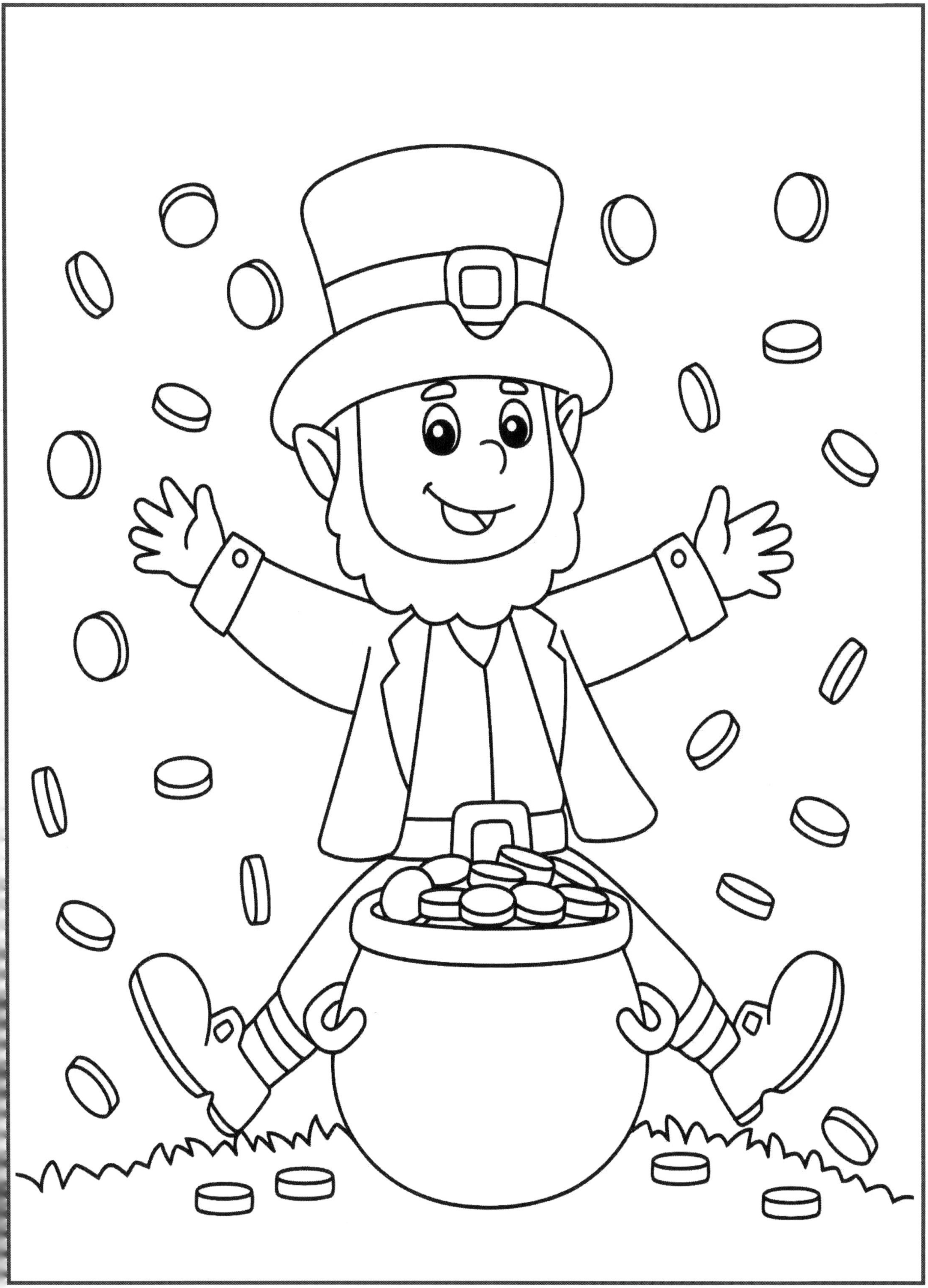

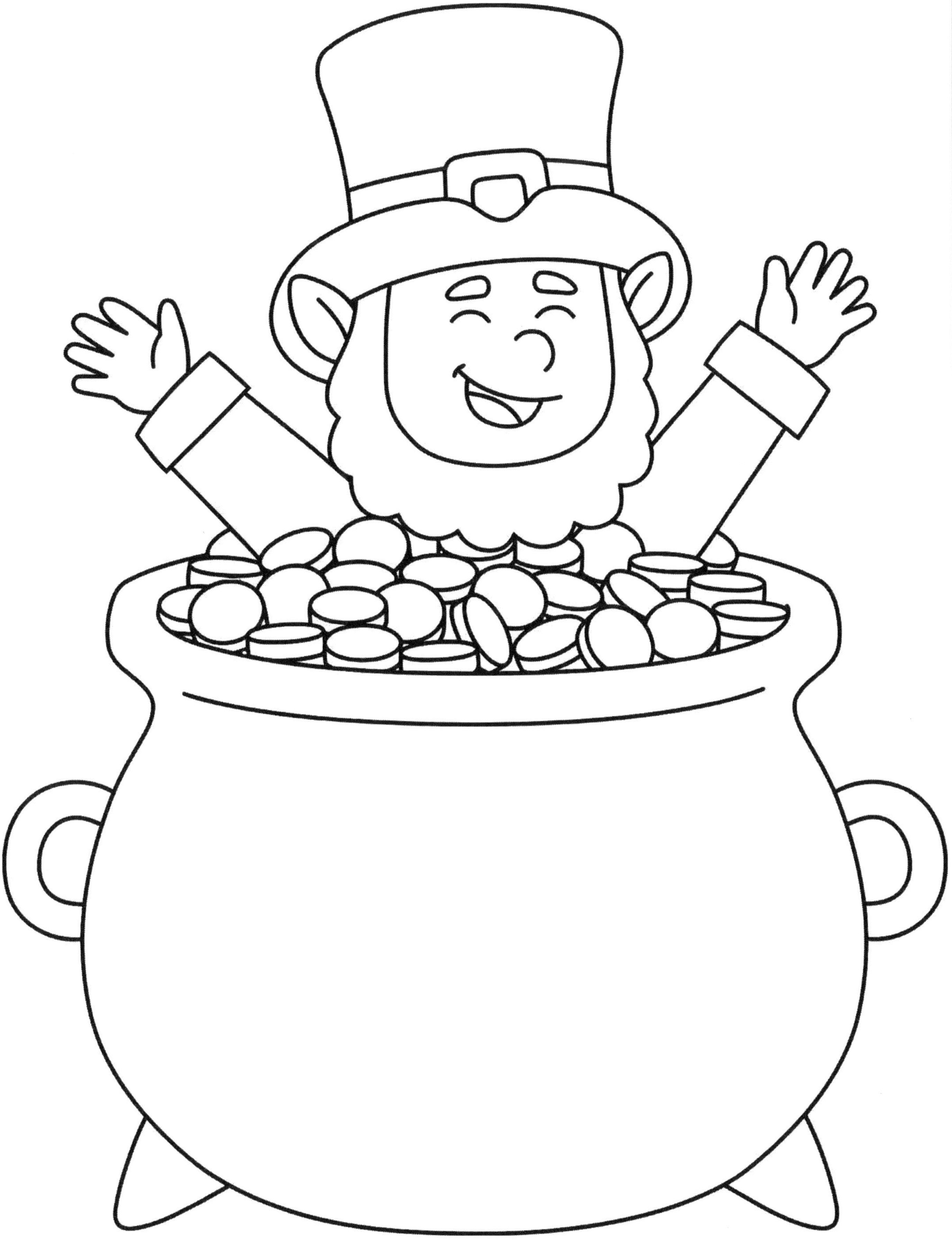

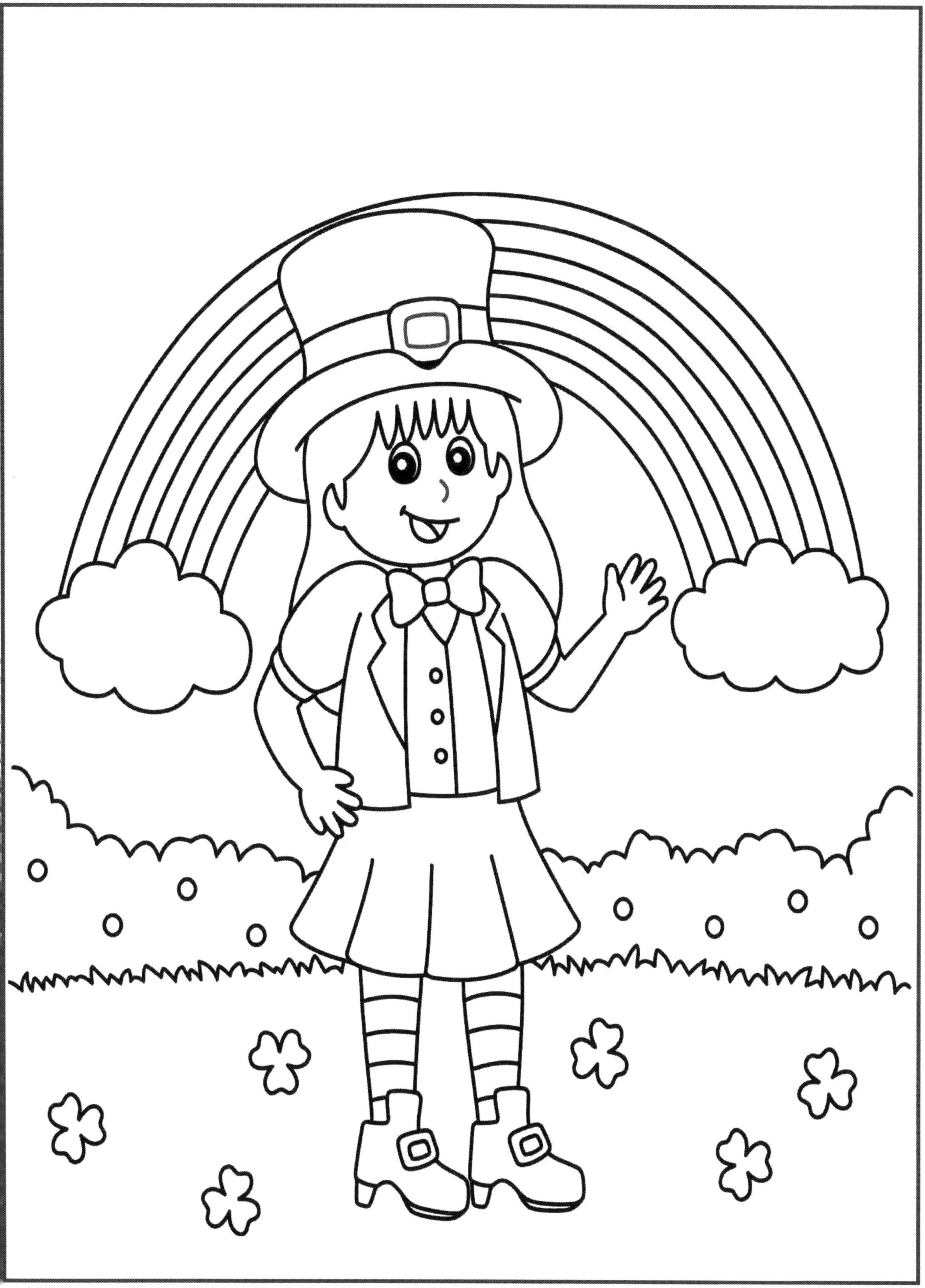

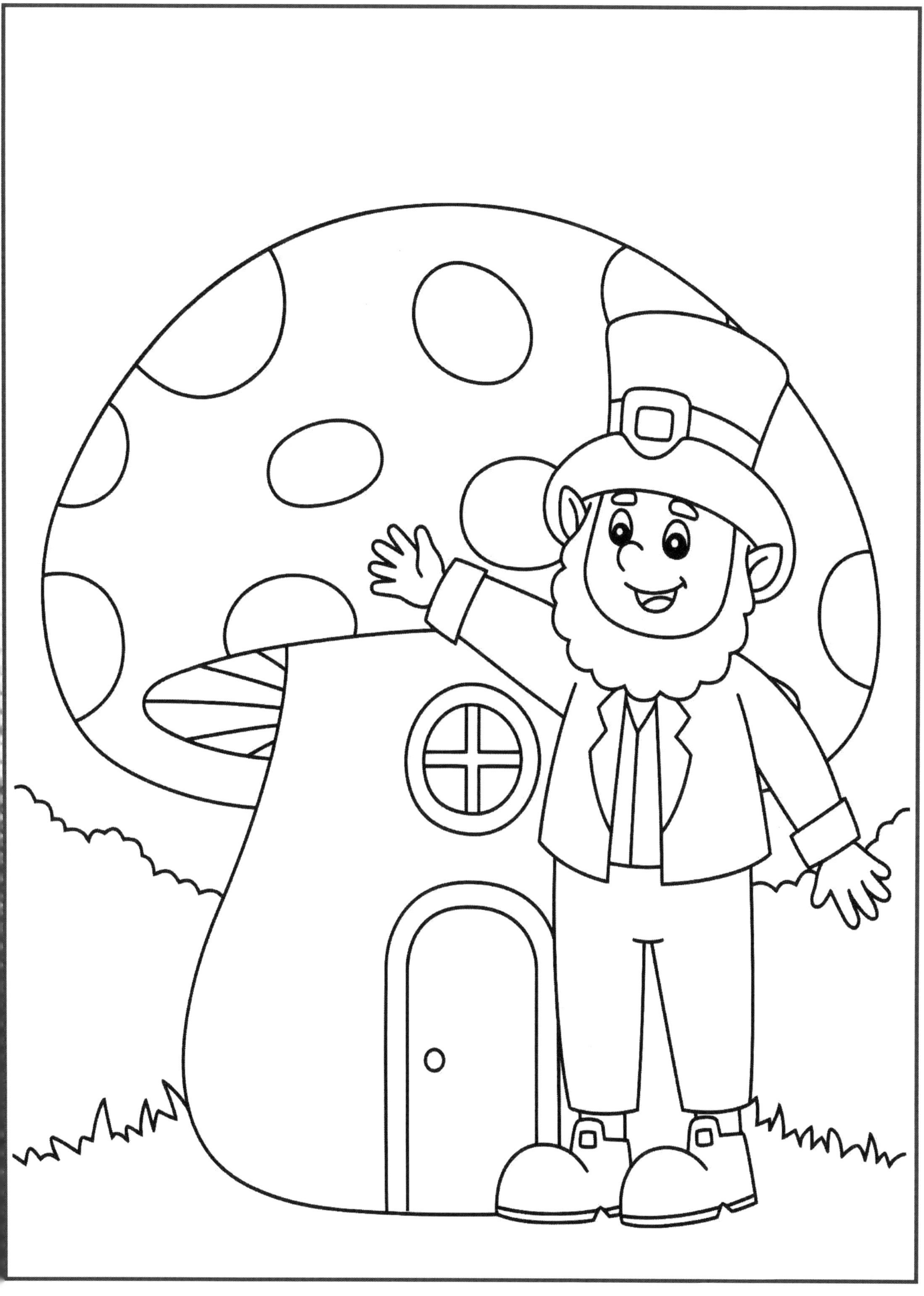

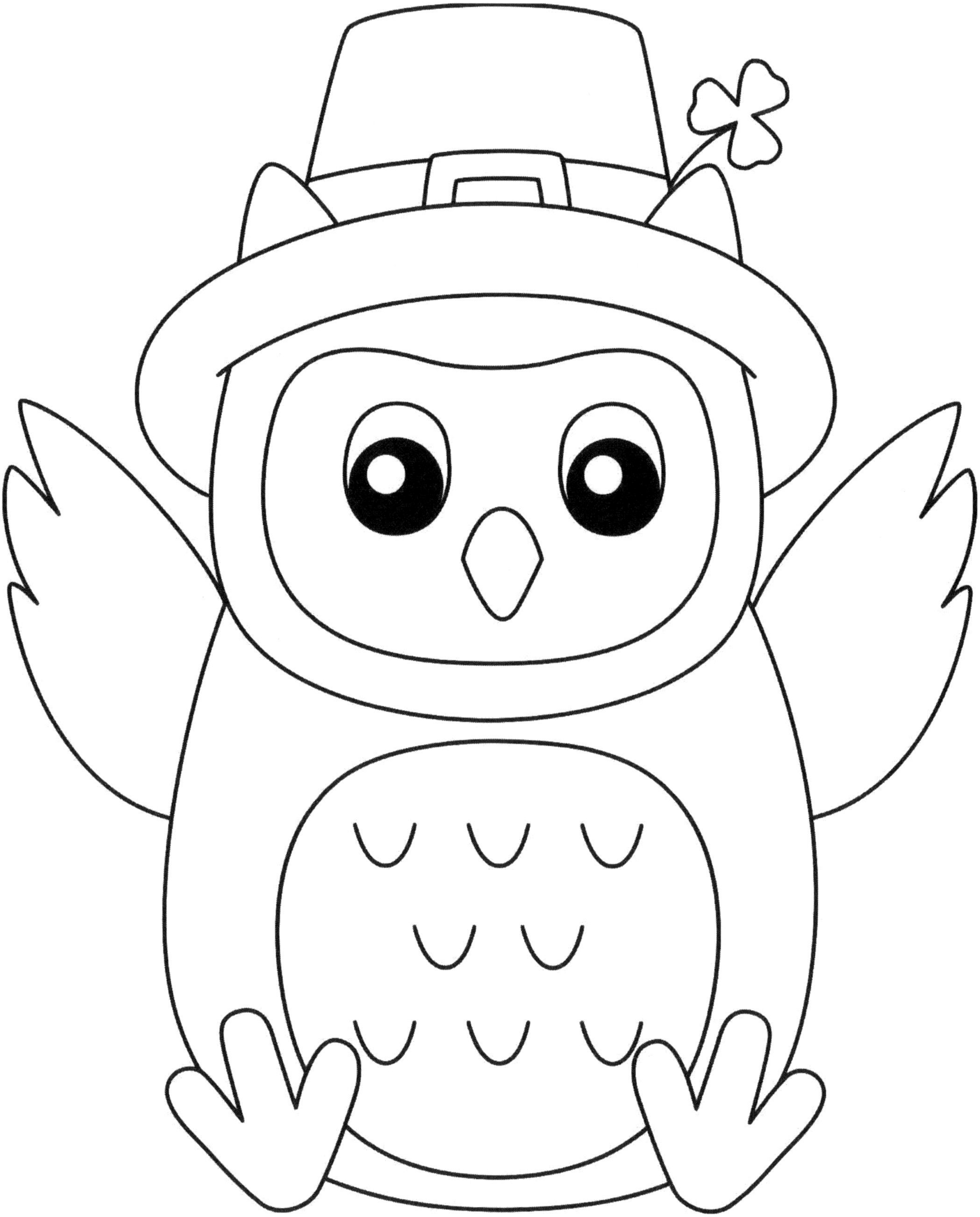

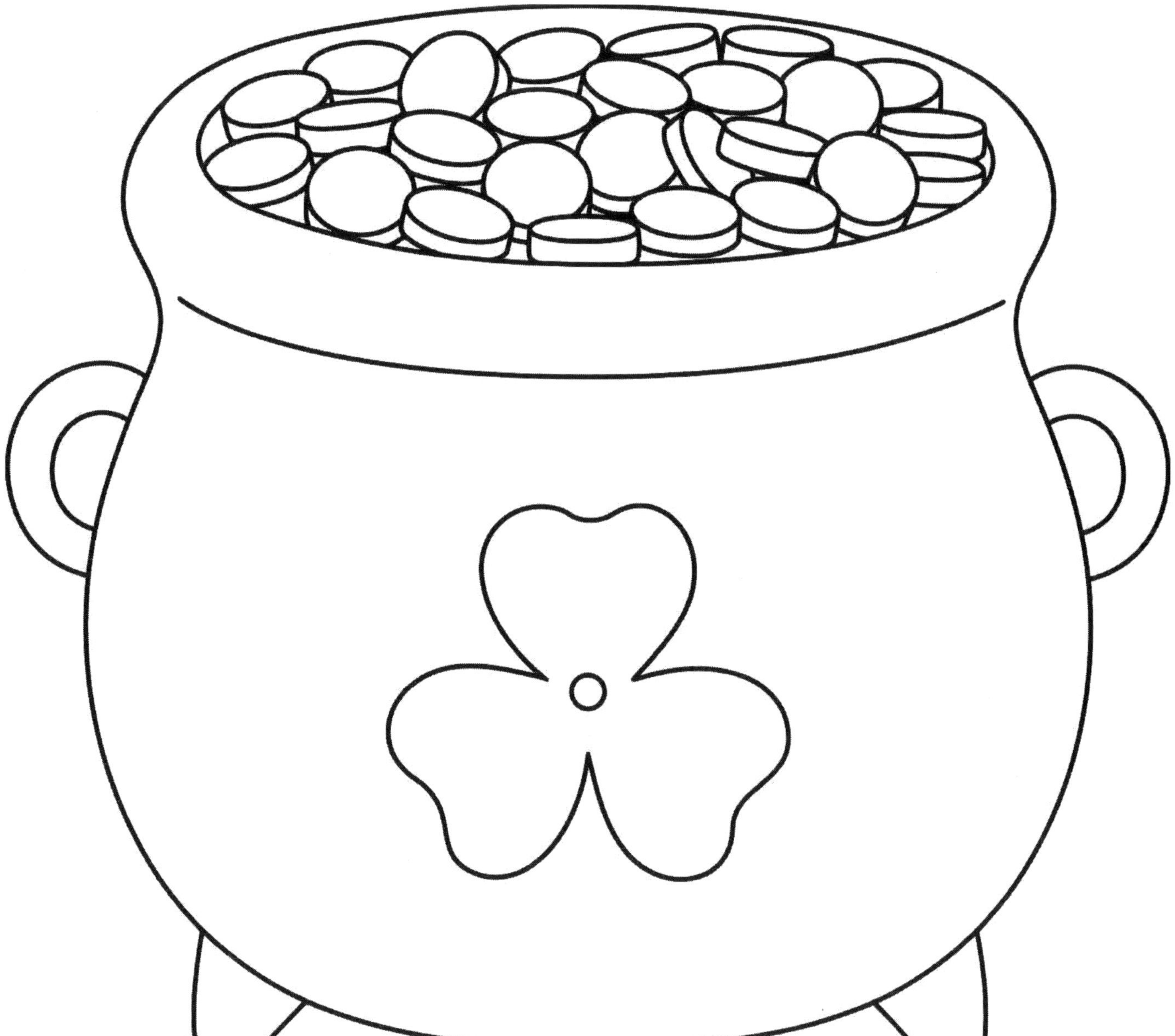

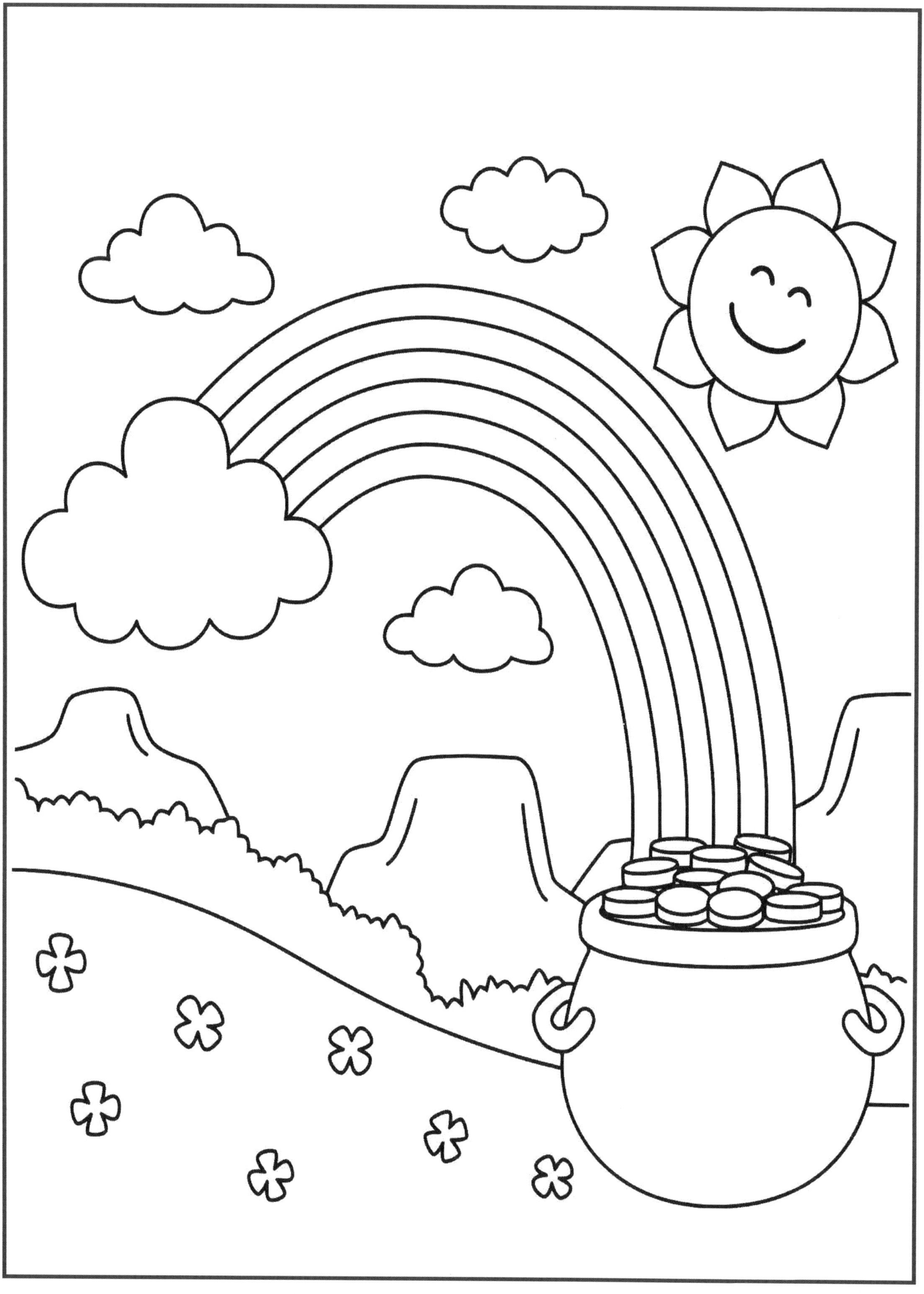

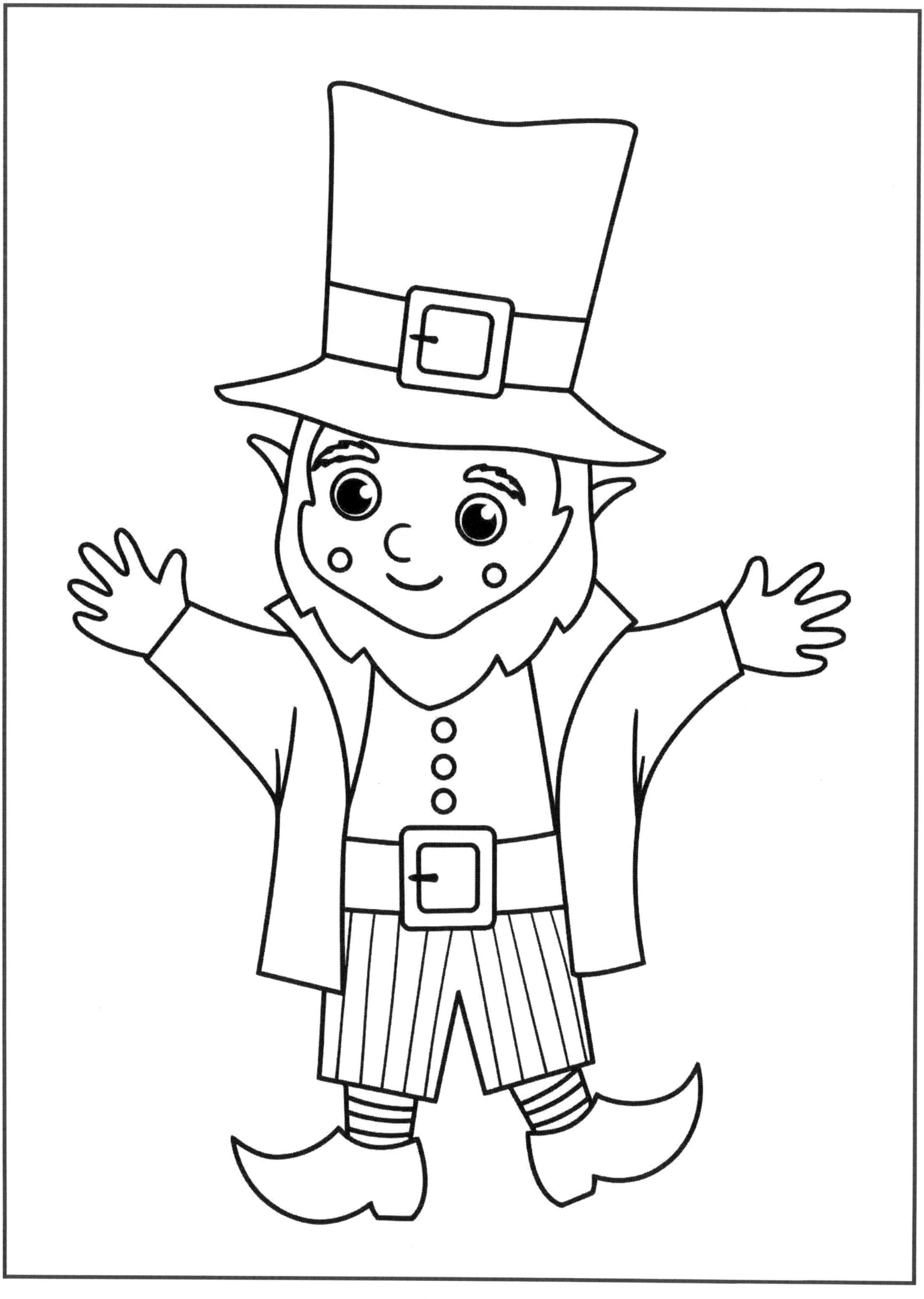

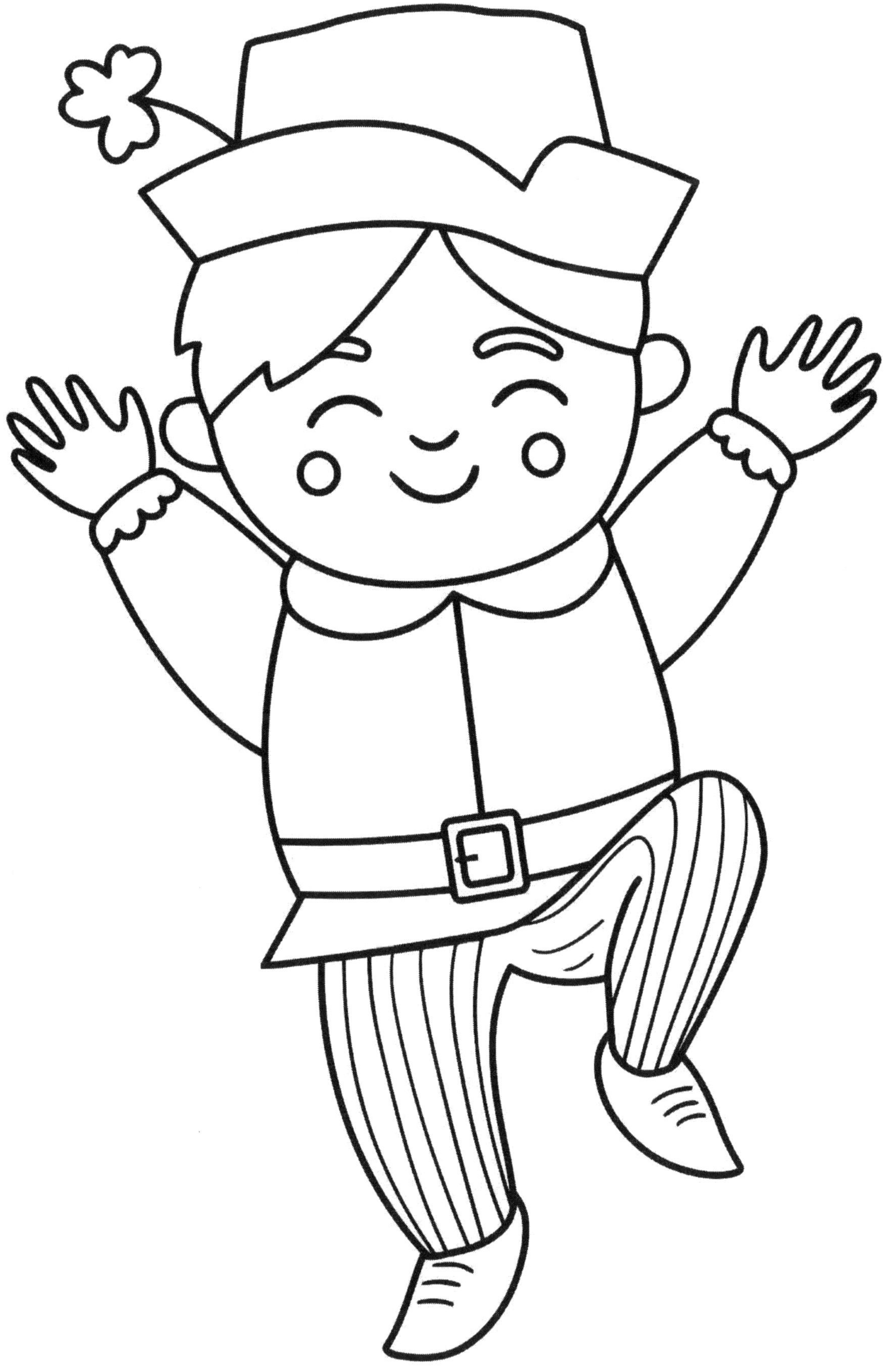

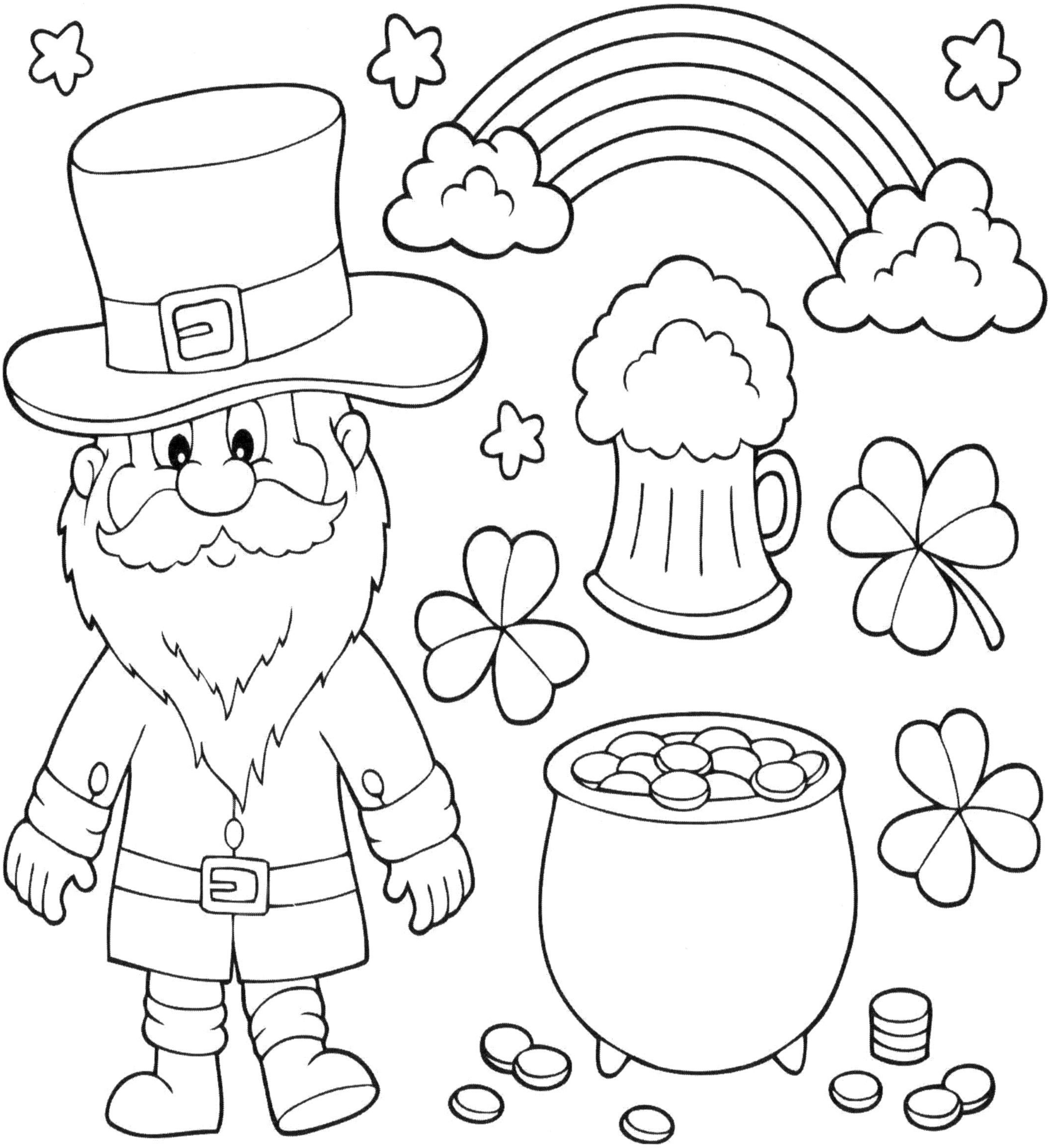

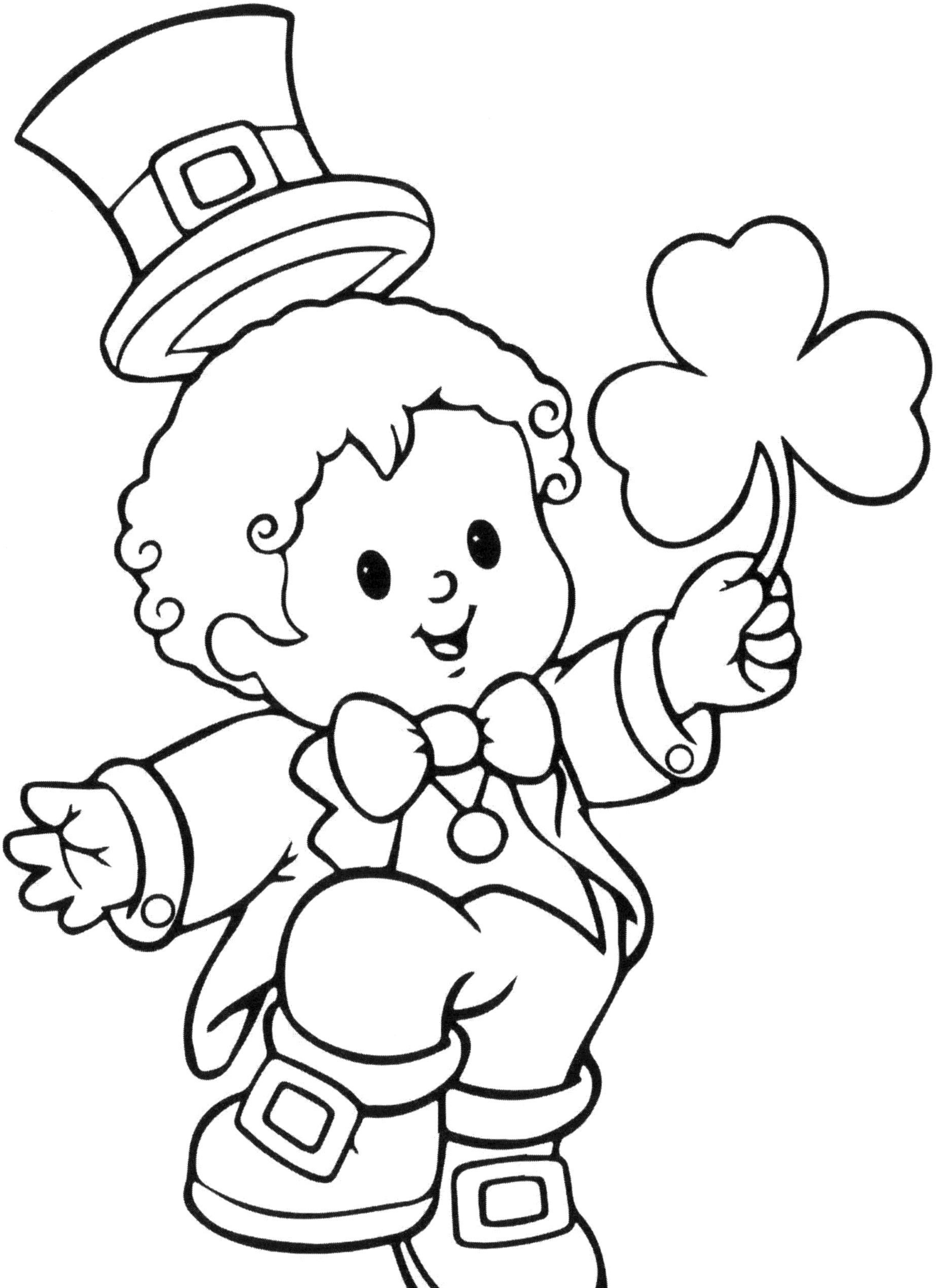

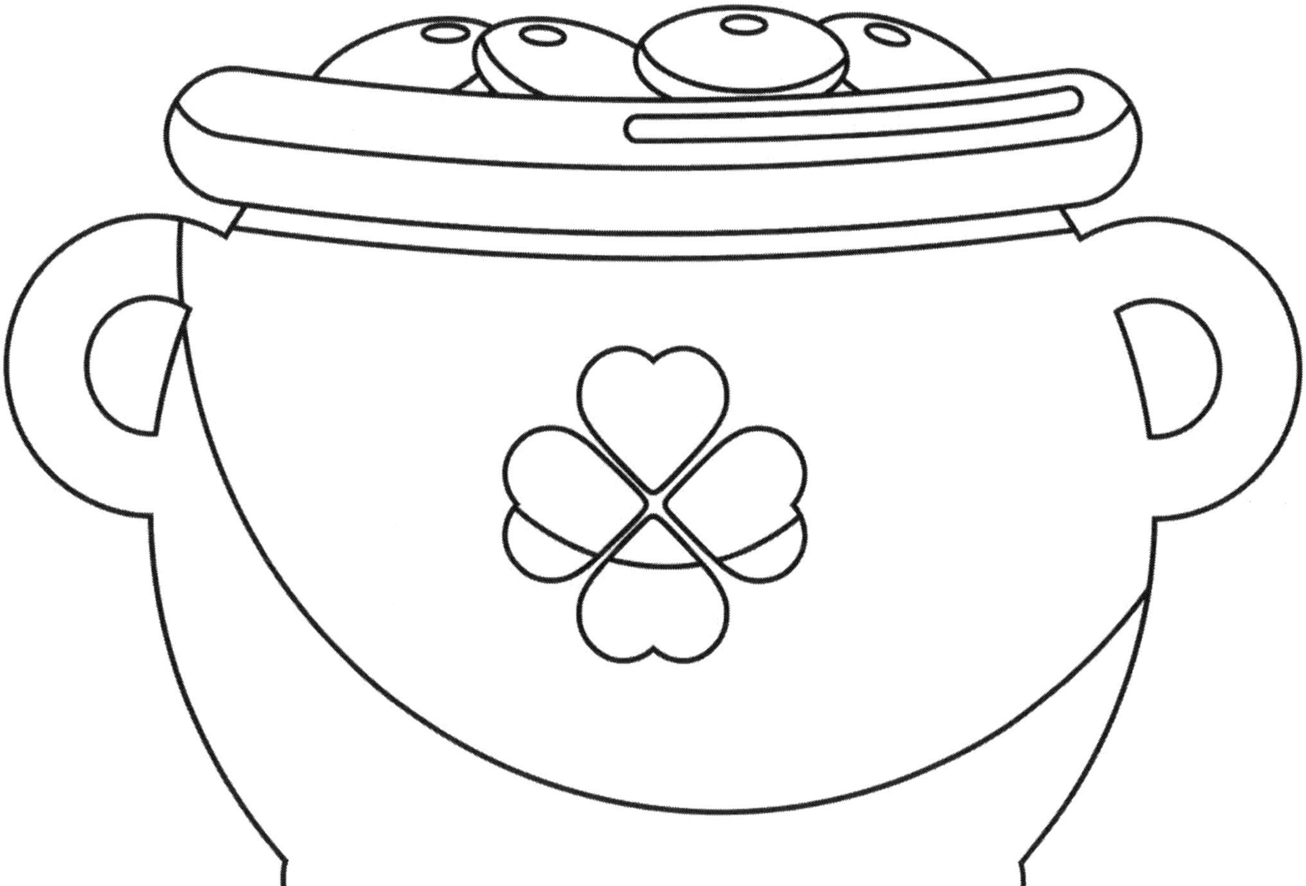

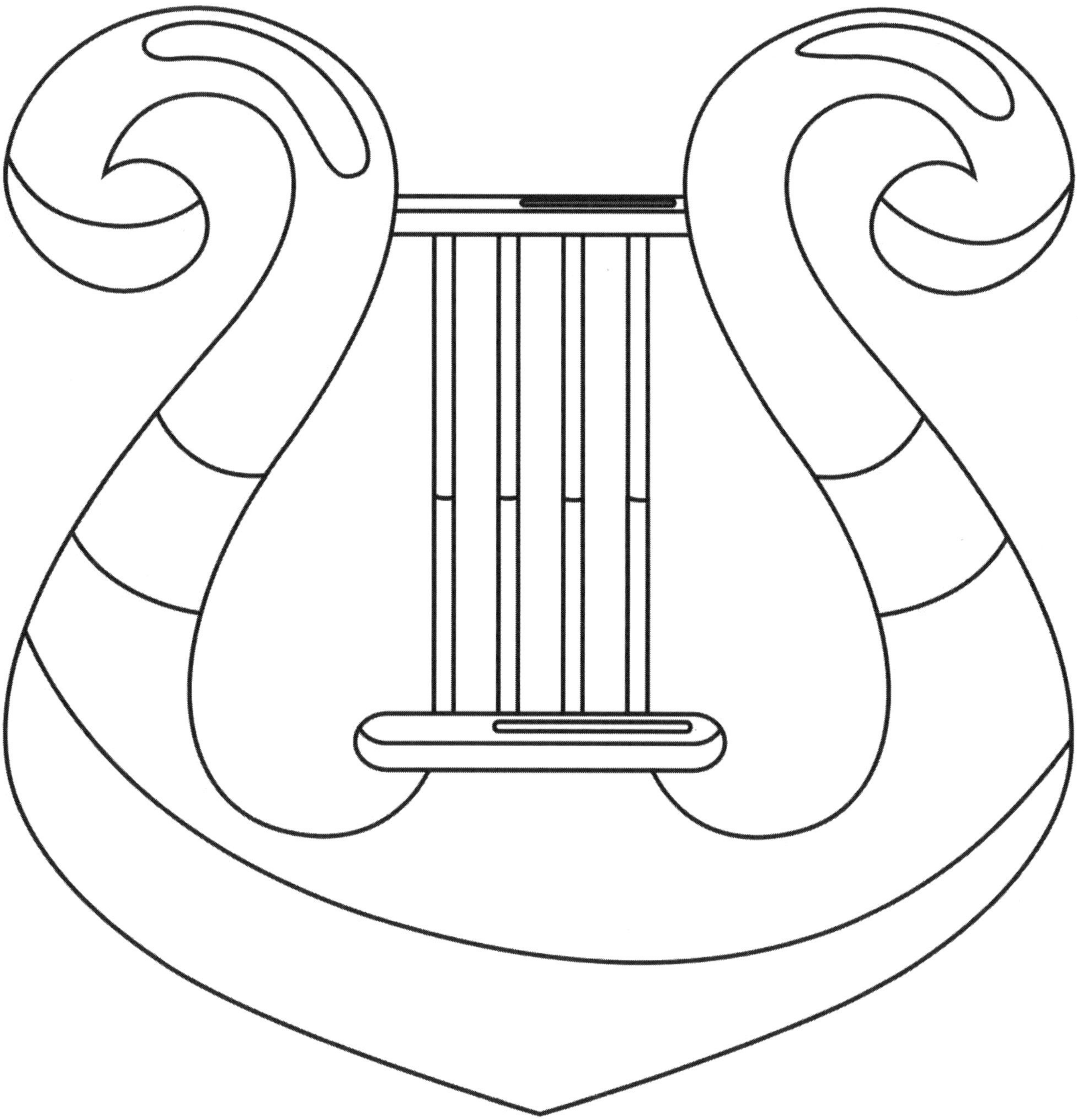

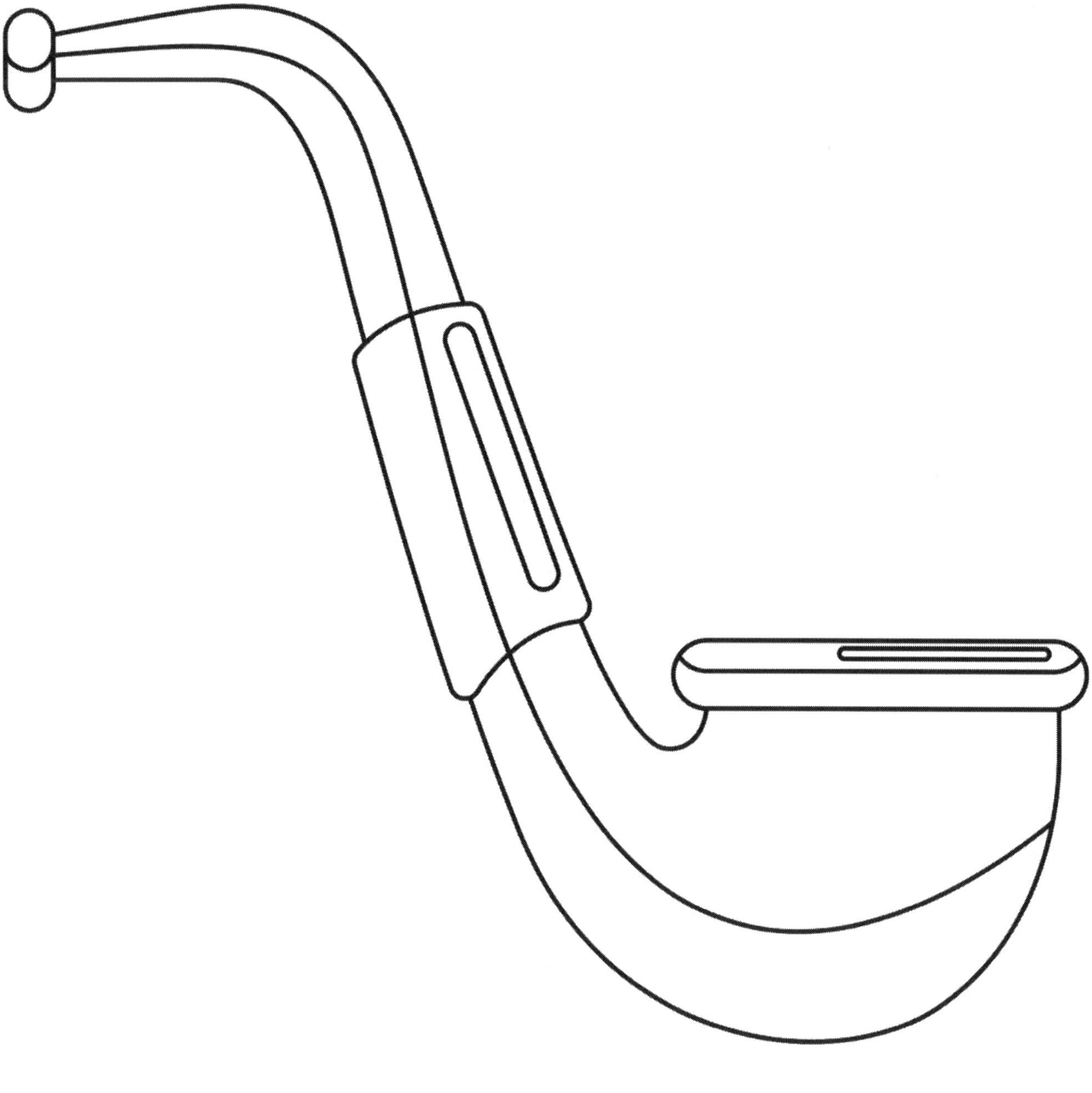

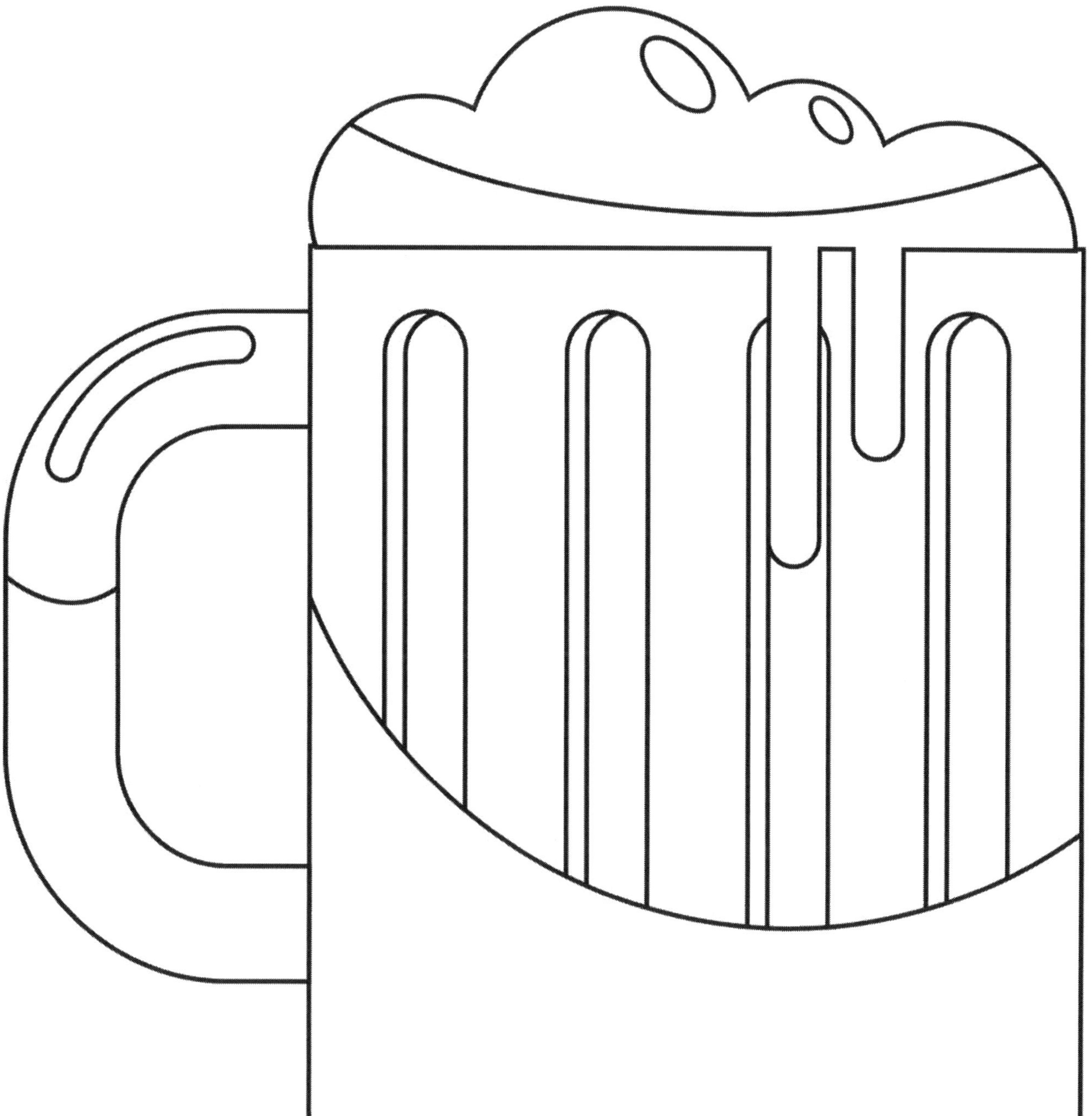

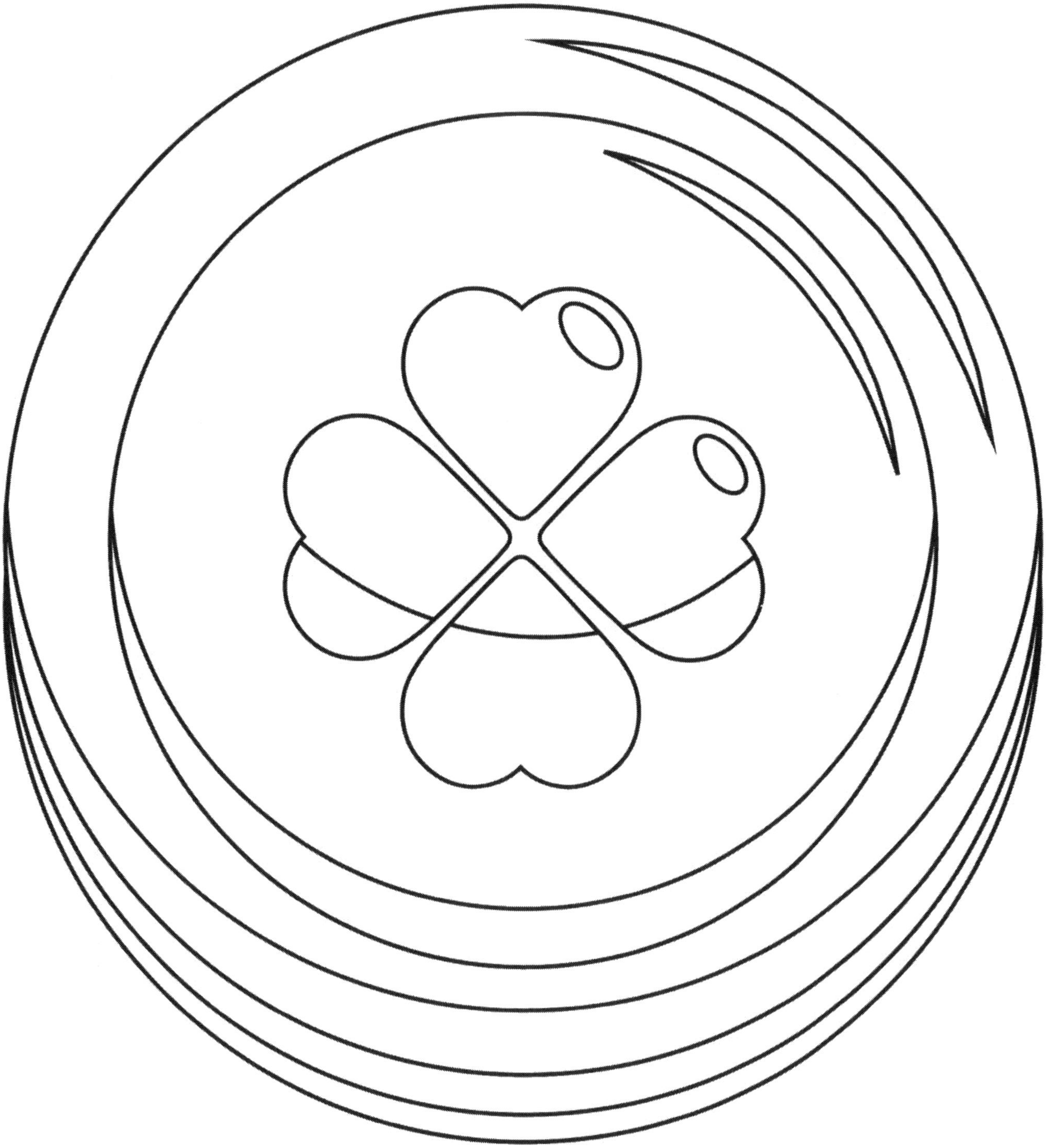

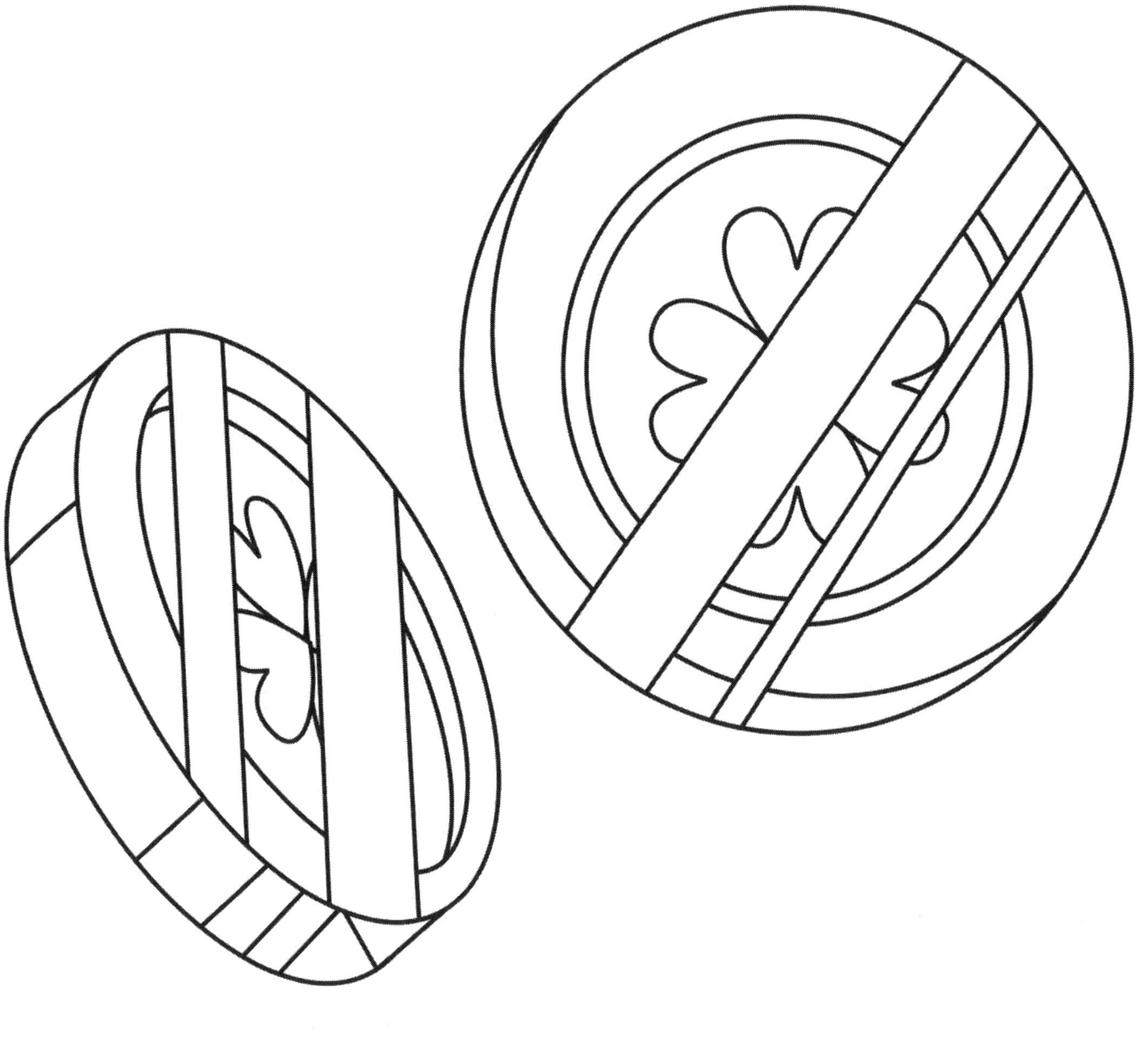

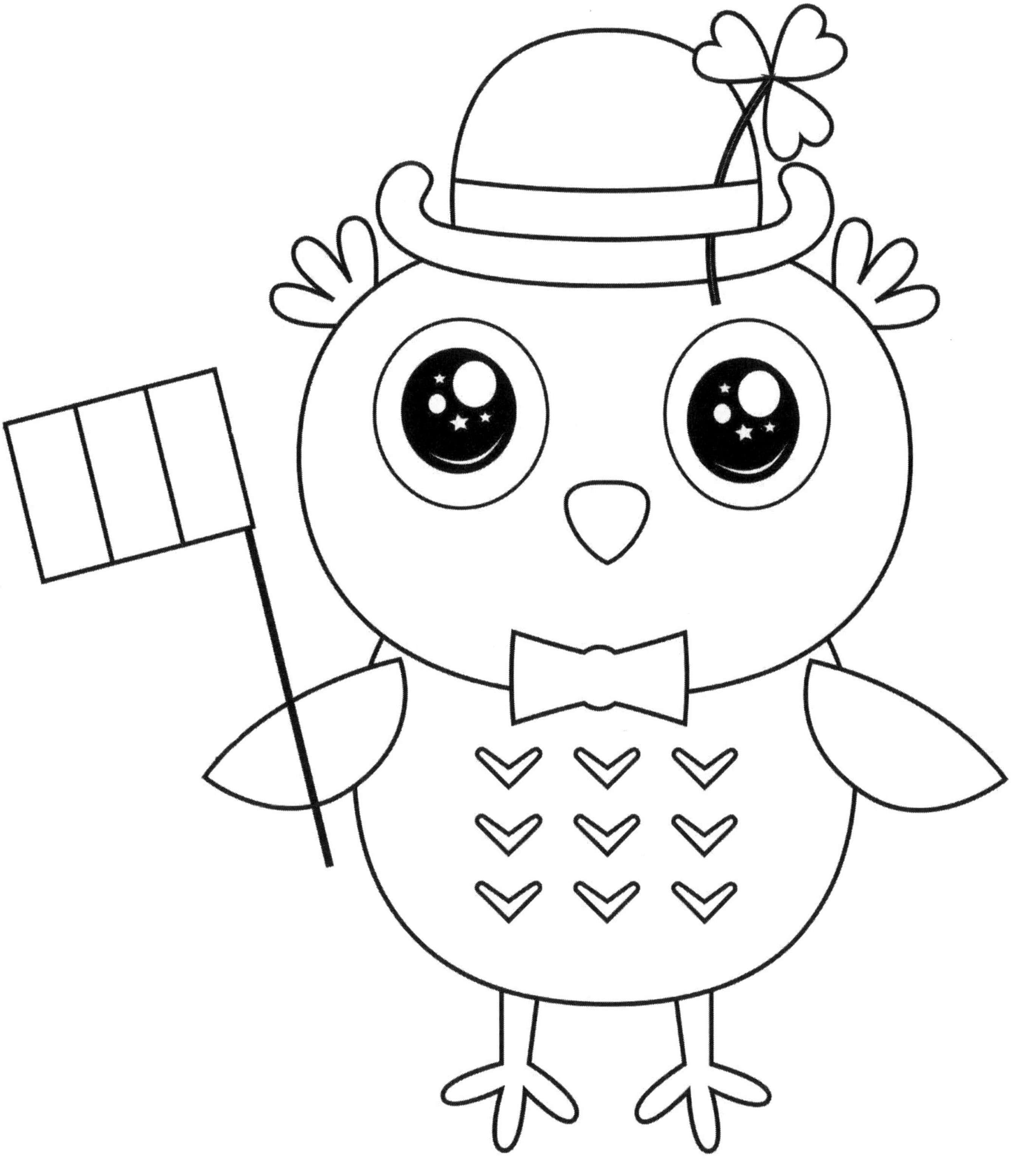

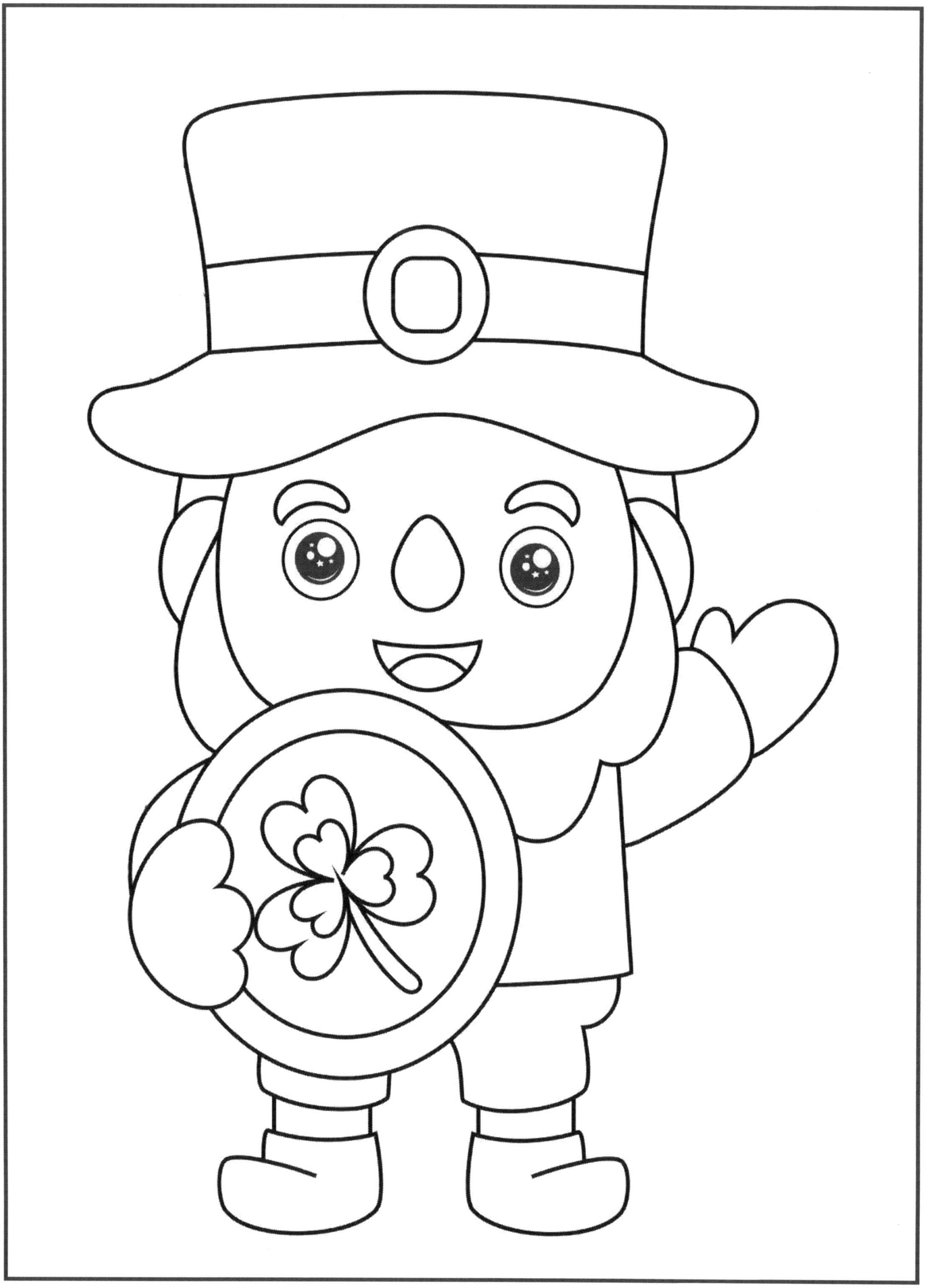

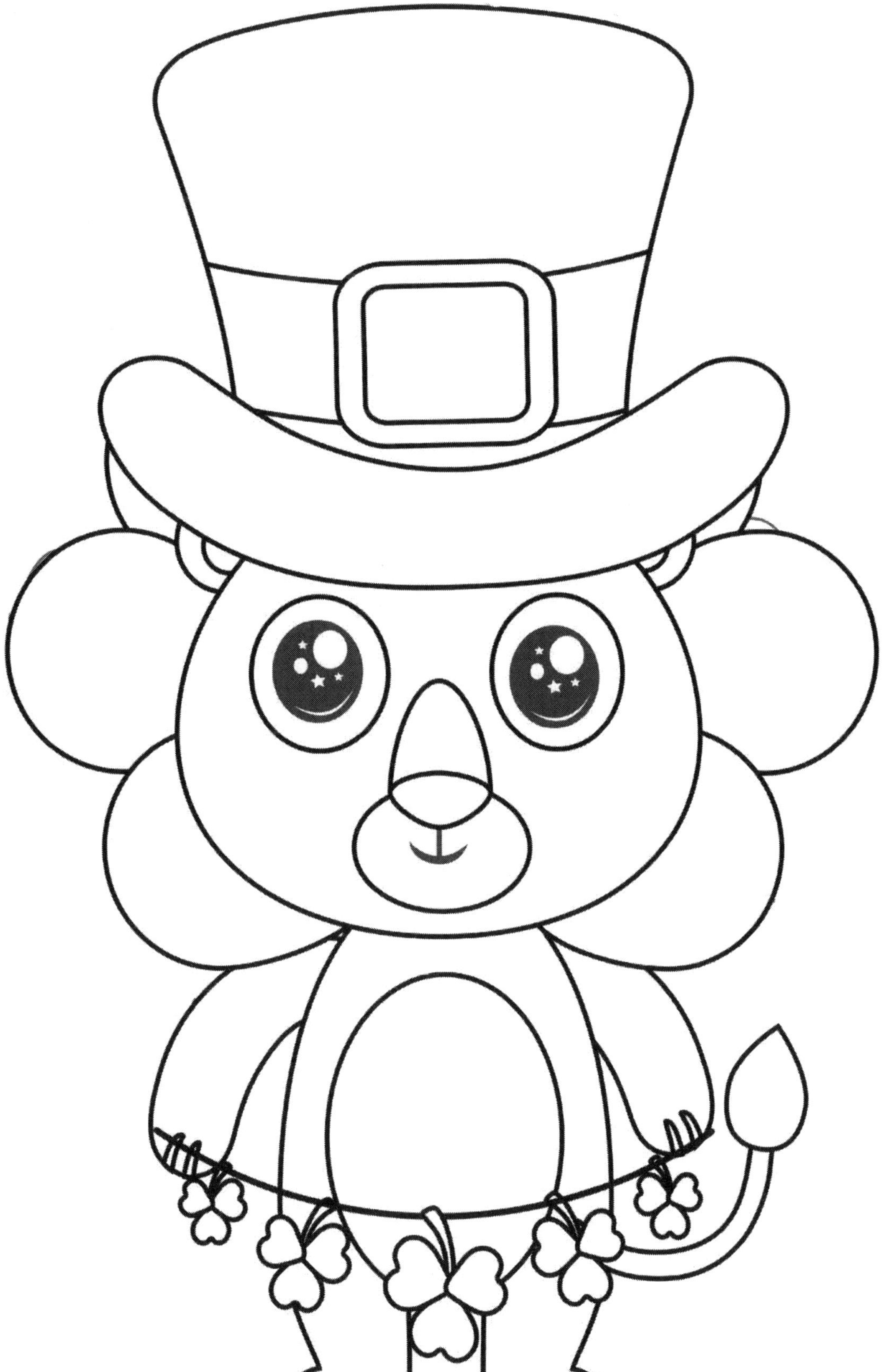

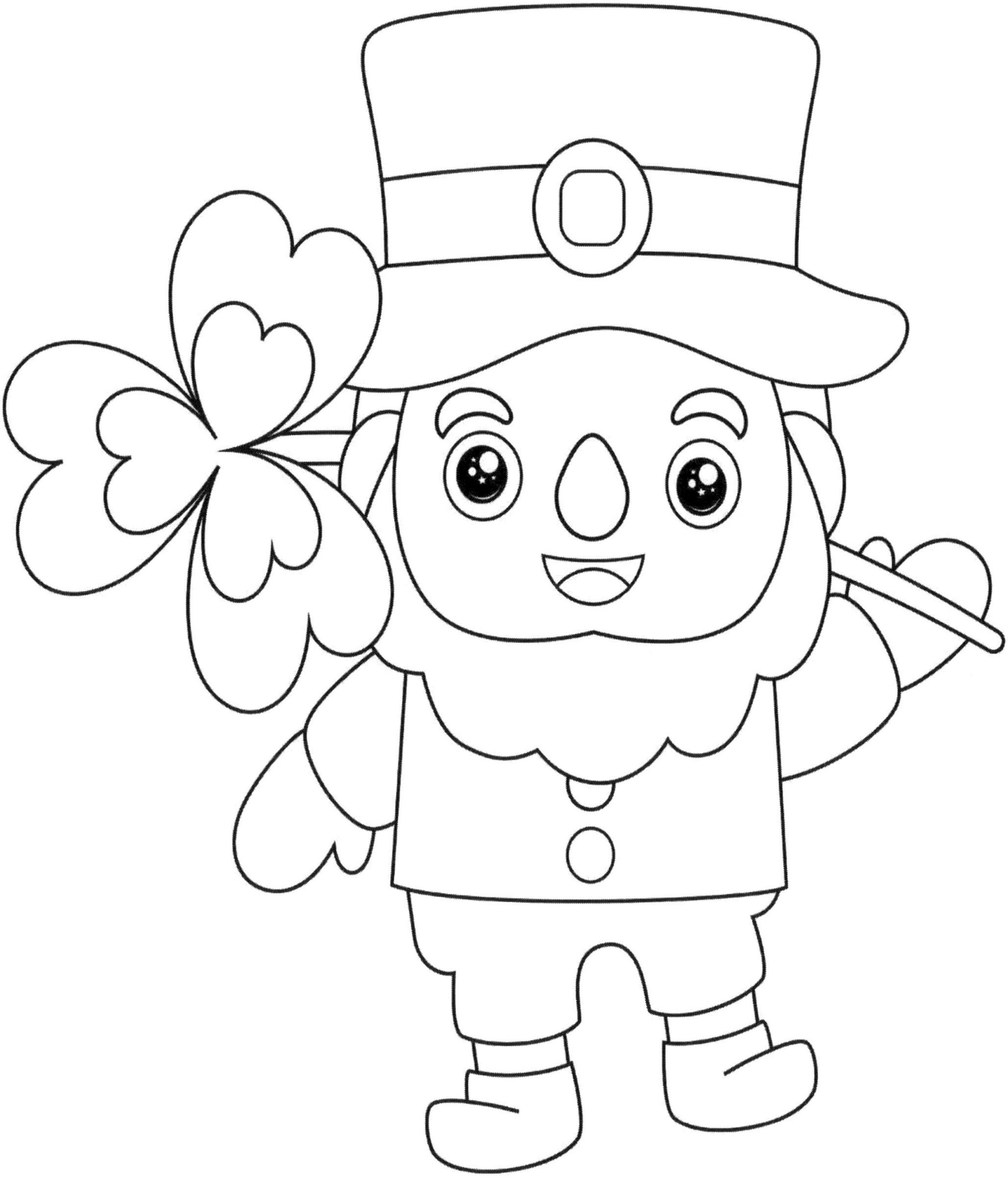

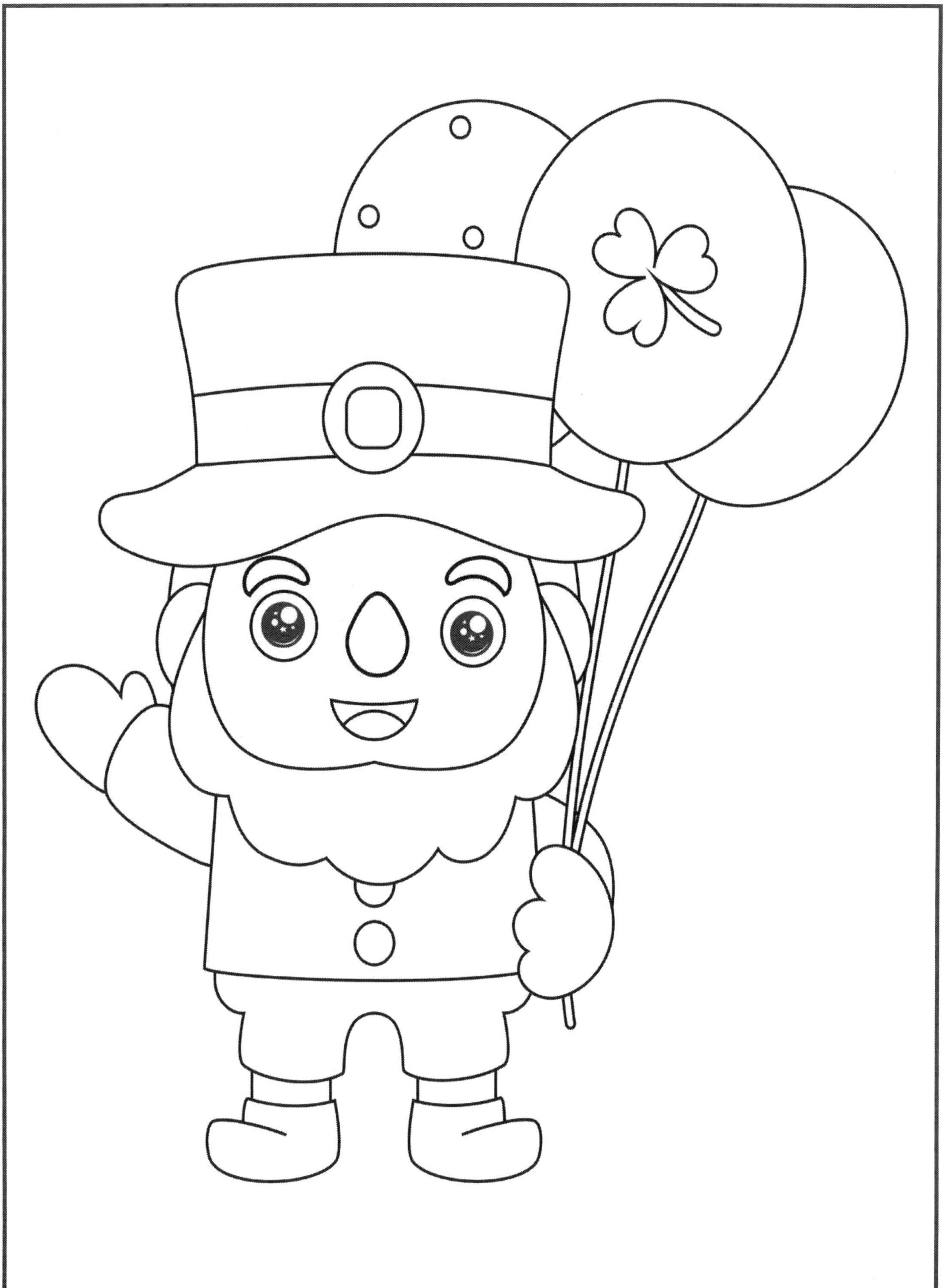

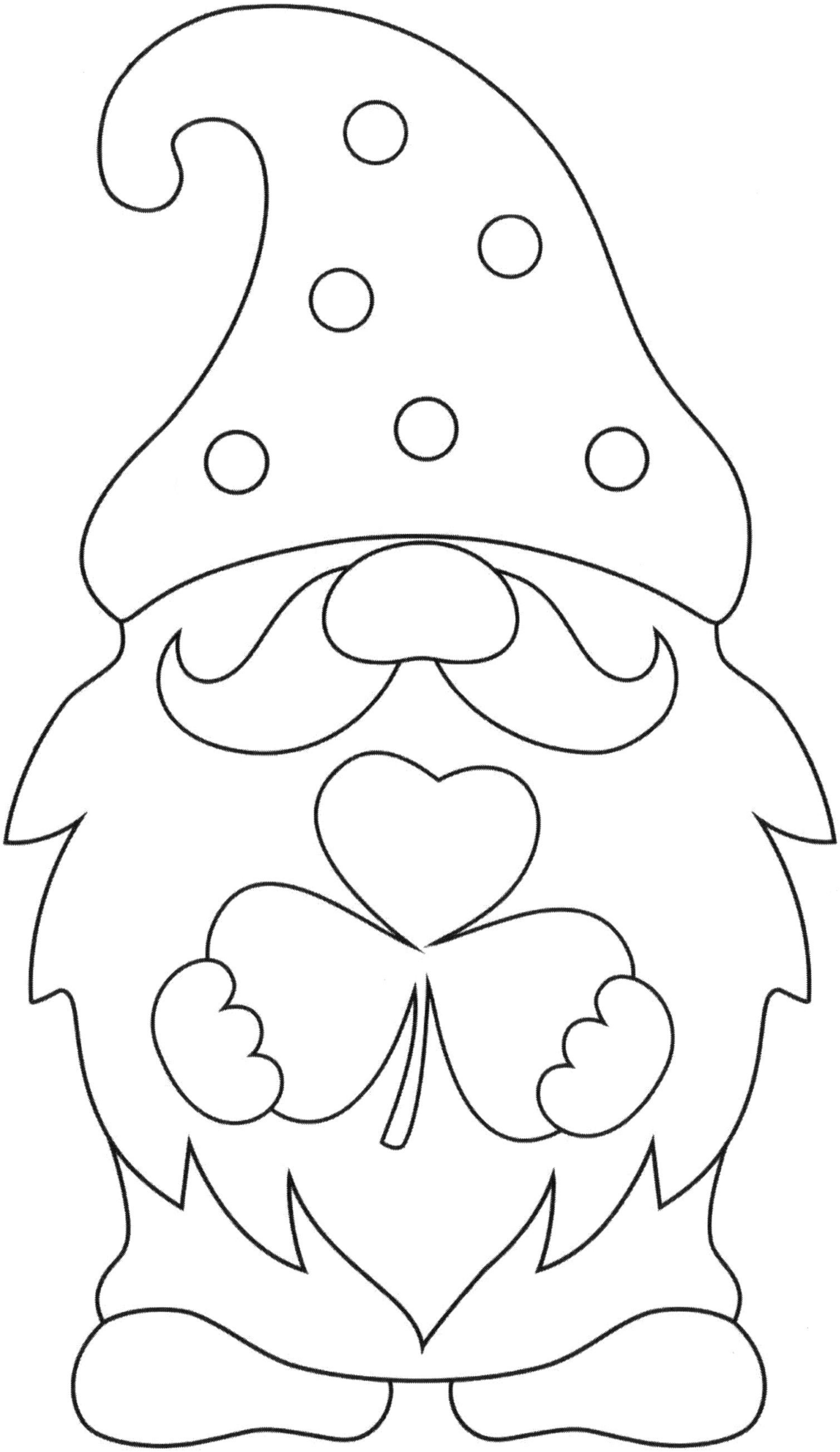

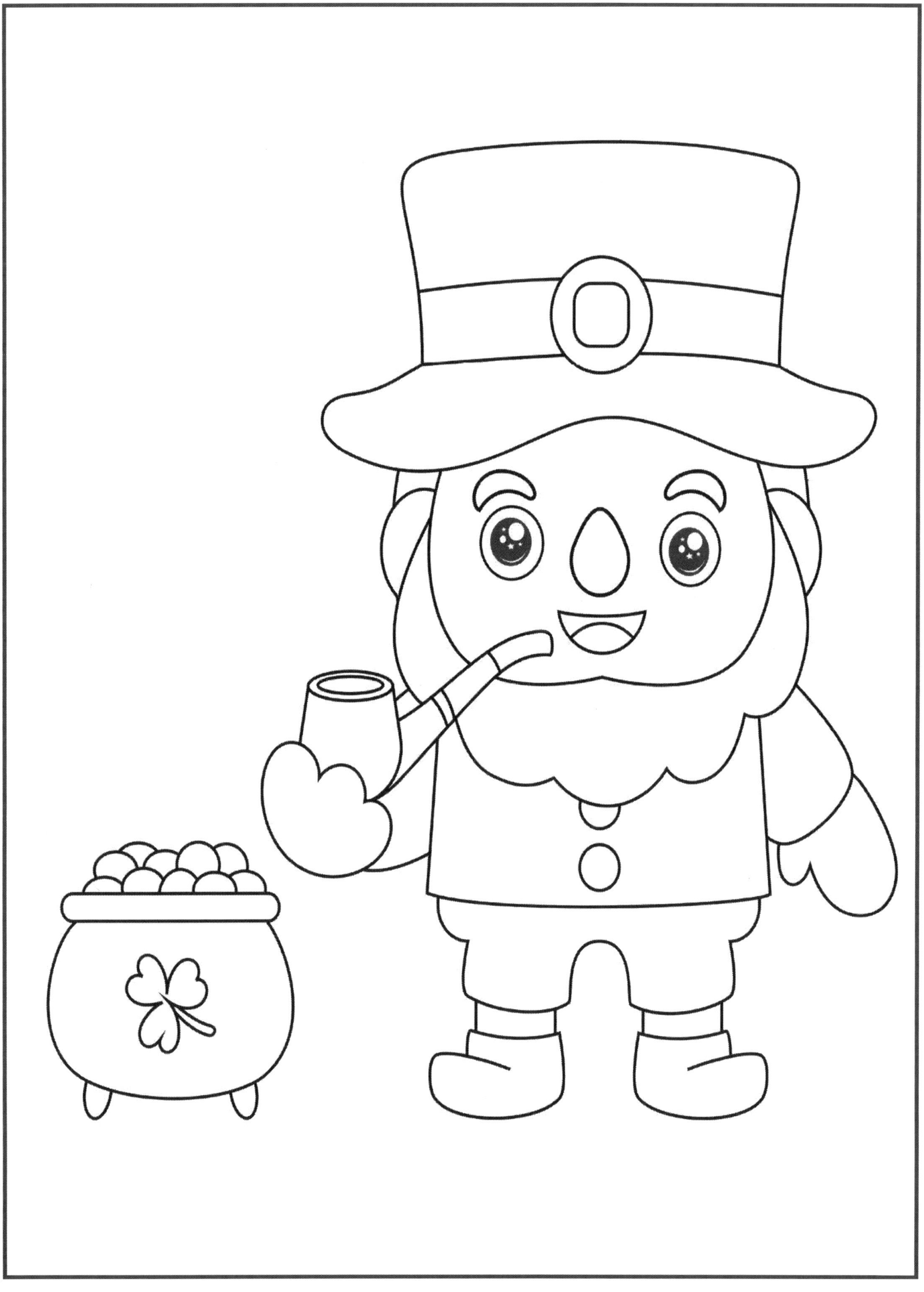

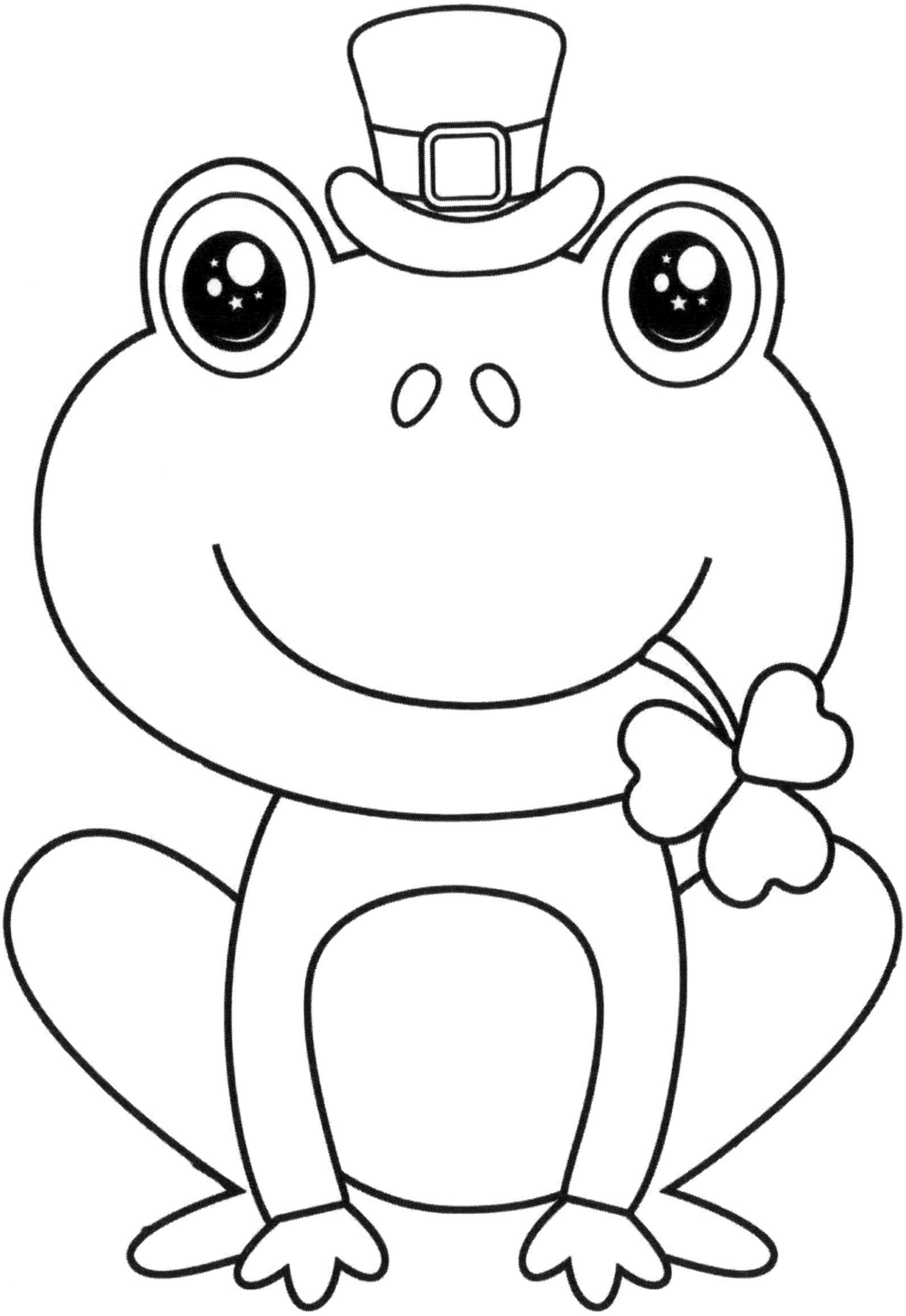

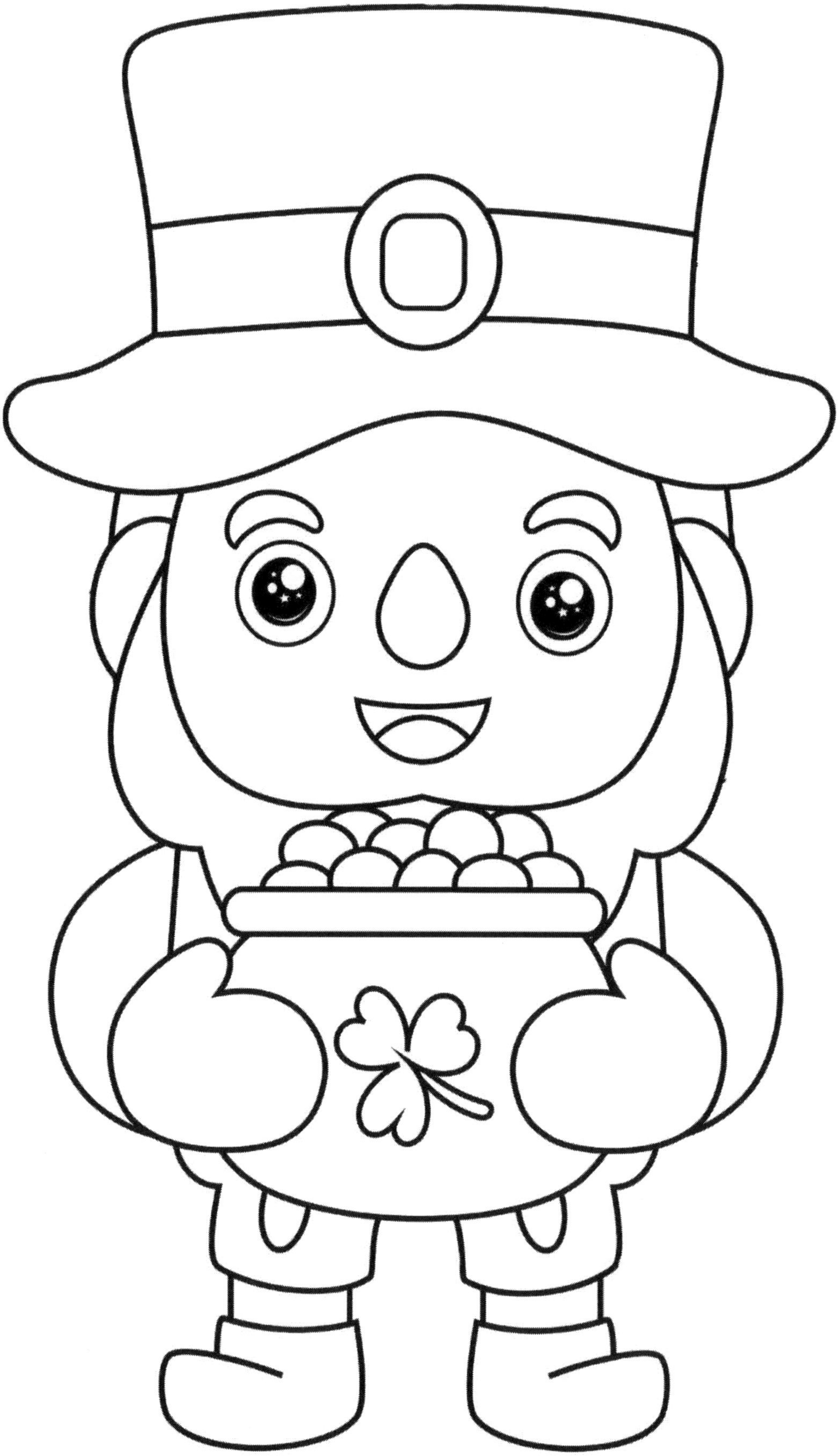

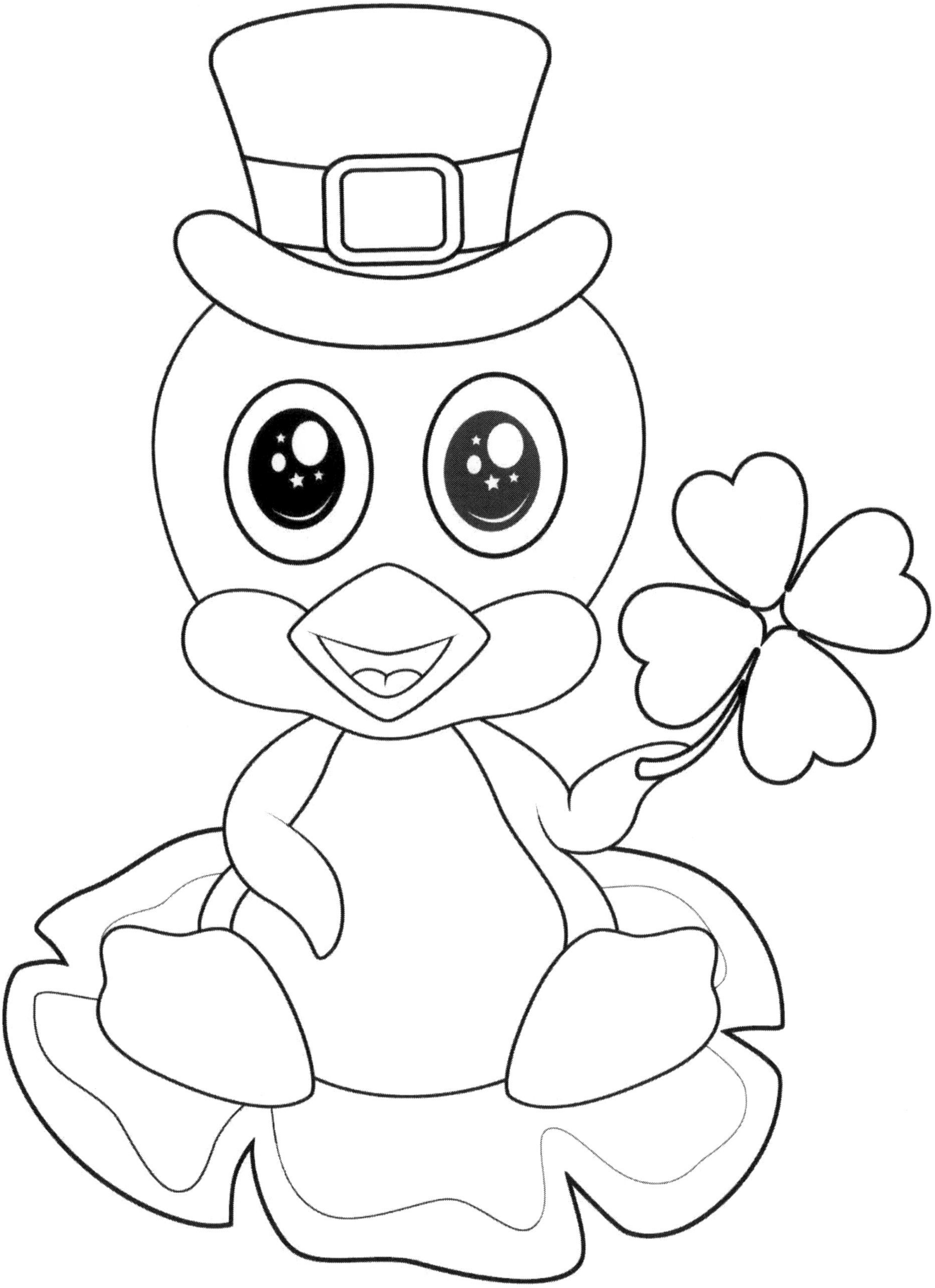

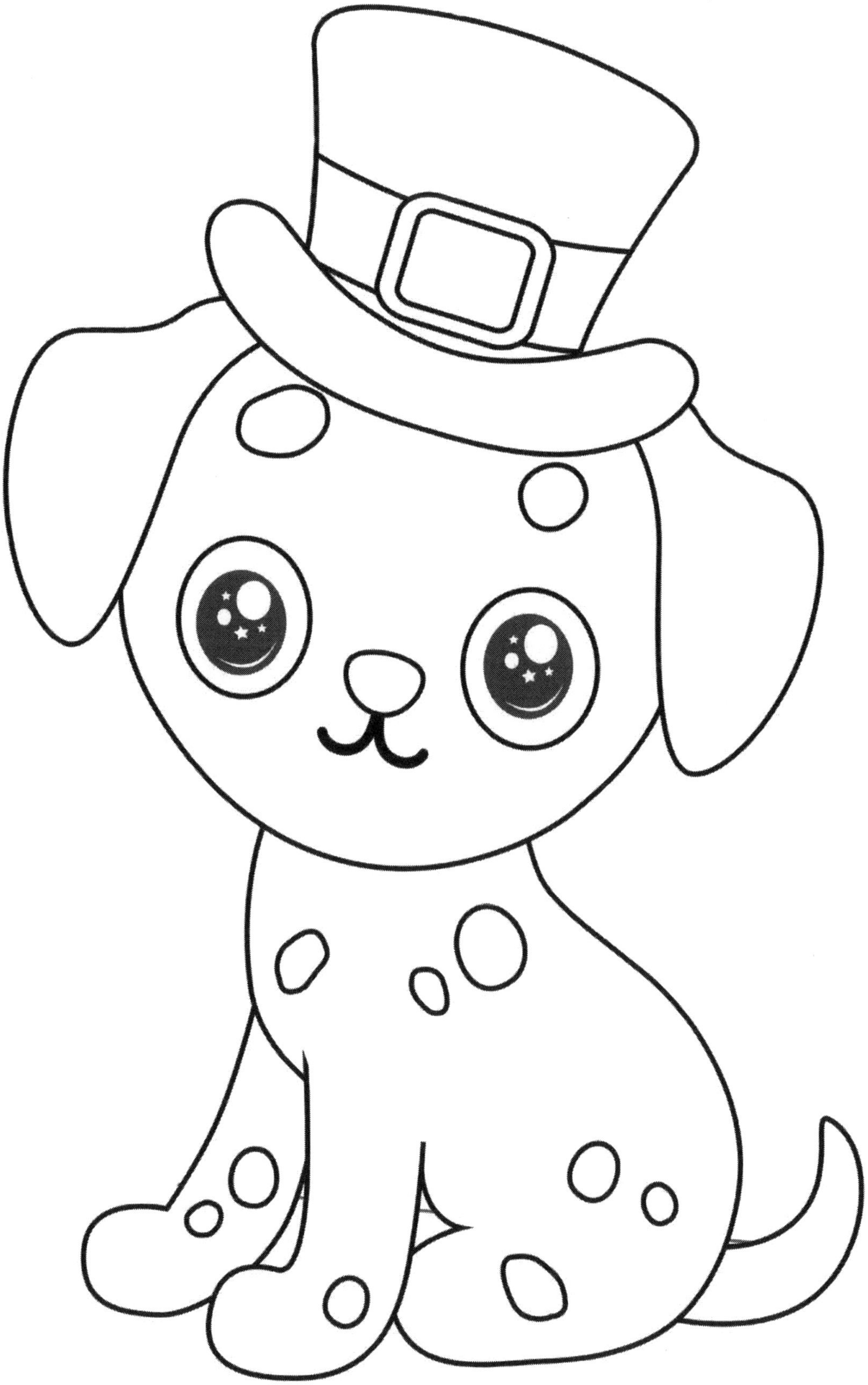

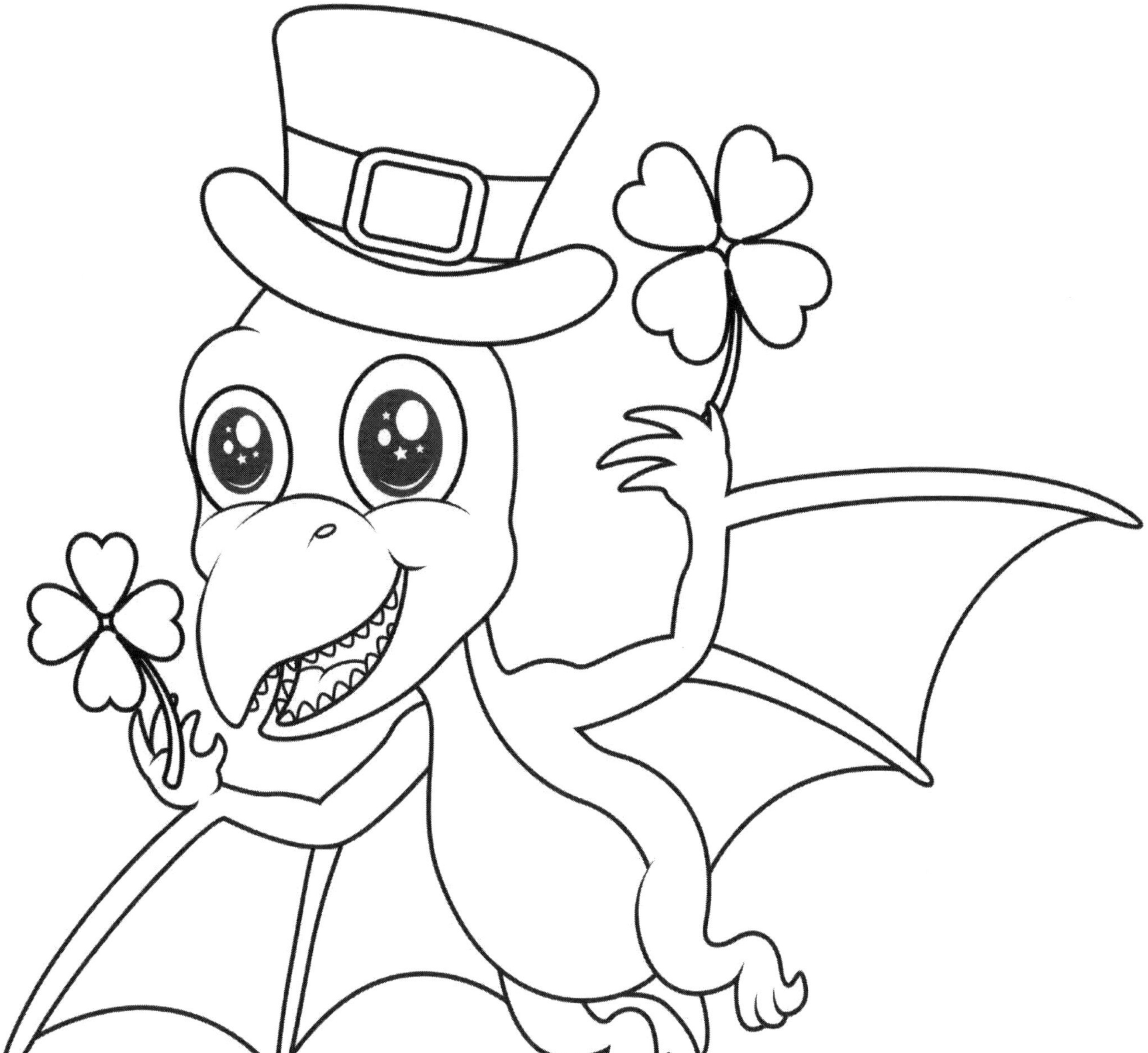

Made in the USA
Las Vegas, NV
02 March 2024

86618126R00057